S0-AXY-564

Praise for
The True Cost of Happiness

"From our investment choices to our spending choices to the things we teach and don't teach our children about money, the ways in which we handle our finances are simply a reflection of our beliefs and values. In order to live fulfilling lives, we must be sure that our financial choices—whether we're talking about personal finance, corporate behavior, or social behavior—represent who we really are, and who we really want to be. This book shows us how to do that."

—Arthur R. Hogan III
Managing Director
Chief Investment Strategist
Jefferies & Company, Inc.

"The biggest single mistake that people make with their finances—and, often, their lives—is to ignore or forget their most cherished goals. This book not only promotes financial literacy and great financial decisions; it can be the first step toward a really terrific life."

—Bob Veres

"What make's this work uniquely valuable to the consumer is its focus. First on helping people identify their goals and dreams, and then by providing a basic financial roadmap for financing those goals and dreams. A wonderful addition!"

—Martin Siesta, CFP (r), MSFS Registered Life Planner
National Board Member of the Financial Planning Association
Compass Wealth Management

The True Cost of Happiness

THE REAL STORY BEHIND MANAGING YOUR MONEY

Stacey Tisdale
Paula Boyer Kennedy

John Wiley & Sons, Inc.

Copyright © 2007 by Stacey Tisdale and Paula Boyer Kennedy. All rights reserved.

Published by John Wiley & Sons, Inc., Hoboken, New Jersey.
Published simultaneously in Canada.

Wiley Bicentennial Logo: Richard J. Pacifico

No part of this publication may be reproduced, stored in a retrieval system, or transmitted in any form or by any means, electronic, mechanical, photocopying, recording, scanning, or otherwise, except as permitted under Section 107 or 108 of the 1976 United States Copyright Act, without either the prior written permission of the Publisher, or authorization through payment of the appropriate per-copy fee to the Copyright Clearance Center, Inc., 222 Rosewood Drive, Danvers, MA 01923, (978) 750-8400, fax (978) 646-8600, or on the Web at www.copyright.com. Requests to the Publisher for permission should be addressed to the Permissions Department, John Wiley & Sons, Inc., 111 River Street, Hoboken, NJ 07030, (201) 748-6011, fax (201) 748-6008, or online at www.wiley.com/go/permissions.

Limit of Liability/Disclaimer of Warranty: While the publisher and author have used their best efforts in preparing this book, they make no representations or warranties with respect to the accuracy or completeness of the contents of this book and specifically disclaim any implied warranties of merchantability or fitness for a particular purpose. No warranty may be created or extended by sales representatives or written sales materials. The advice and strategies contained herein may not be suitable for your situation. You should consult with a professional where appropriate. Neither the publisher nor author shall be liable for any loss of profit or any other commercial damages, including but not limited to special, incidental, consequential, or other damages.

For general information on our other products and services or for technical support, please contact our Customer Care Department within the United States at (800) 762-2974, outside the United States at (317) 572-3993, or fax (317) 572-4002.

Wiley also publishes its books in a variety of electronic formats. Some content that appears in print may not be available in electronic formats. For more information about Wiley products, visit our Web site at www.wiley.com.

Library of Congress Cataloging-in-Publication Data:

Tisdale, Stacey, 1966–
  The true cost of happiness : the real story behind managing your money / Stacey Tisdale and Paula Boyer Kennedy.
    p. cm.
  ISBN 978-0-470-13906-6 (cloth)
  ISBN 978-0-470-49657-2 (paper)
  1. Finance, Personal—Psychological aspects. 2. Awareness. 3. Self-actualization (Psychology) 4. Change (Psychology) I. Kennedy, Paula Boyer, 1956– II. Title.
III. Title: Managing your money.
  HG179.T516 2007
  332.024—dc22

                                                                2007012350

Printed in the United States of America
10 9 8 7 6 5 4 3 2 1

Contents

Part II: The Numbers

Part III: Staying on Course

Acknowledgments

Stacey Tisdale

I'd like to thank my teachers:

To my mom, Jettie Tisdale: Thank you for teaching me that the teacher and the student, also known as the mother and the child, are one and the same. They reside in our hearts eternally. Nothing changes that. It is the truth itself. You are such a great teacher that they named a school after you!

To my dad, Charles Tisdale: Thank you for teaching me through example how we are to live, laugh, and love. Thank you for teaching me the depth of the love a parent has for a child.

To Mom and Dad together: Thank you for teaching me that that "one special love" really does exist," and that being a parent means climbing inside your child and being their dreams with them.

To my grandmother, Rose Johnson: Thank you for teaching me that faith is really all that you need.

To my husband, Chris: Thank you for teaching me what it truly means to love and care about someone in spite of yourself, and how to show it every second of every day.

To my beloved, beautiful baby boy, Christopher: Thank you for teaching me that love is simply effortless perfection, and that we're born knowing that. We have everything we need to be happy all of the time!

To "Grandpa T," "Grandma Mimi," Jan (aka "Aunt Sister"), Aunt Perri, and Aunt Ann (my husband's family): Thank you for teaching me how loving, honorable, and elegant people can truly be.

To Rudrani: There aren't words.

To Peter Smits: Thank you for teaching me how to be aware.

To Priscilla Shanks: Thank you for teaching me how important it is to look at ourselves and others from the inside out, not the outside in. You are one of the most important gifts I have ever received.

To Sally Kempton: Thank you for teaching me that duality does not exist.

To Muktananda: Thank you for teaching me to remember what I am.

To Eckhart Tolle: Wow!

To Christopher Reeve: Thank you for teaching me that Superman lives in all of us, and for being the living example we needed. You have brought so many wonderful people and experiences into my life.

To journalists everywhere: Thank you for understanding the power of the truth and truly believing that one of the most important things you can do with your life is to empower people with knowledge. Working in this field and with these people, especially my colleagues and mentors at CBS, MarketWatch, CNN, and Wall Street Journal TV, has been one of the most important learning and growth experiences of my life.

To the people and stories that have inspired me throughout my career as a journalist: Thank you for teaching me that the goodness of the human spirit in its limitless forms is the *real* story.

To all of my beautiful sisters that I found at Marymount College, (yes, especially you, Jen, and the whole Chimblo family): Thank you and your families for teaching me what it means to put differences aside and just love someone. I will never forget how you welcomed me into your lives and hearts. Our friendships are forever.

To my sisters and brothers that I found at St. Maarten: Thank you for teaching me that there's not only more than one way to skin a cat, but also more than one way to live this life at every moment. It was one of the most transformational lessons of my entire life, and a major inspiration for this project.

To Gloris Thomas, Dinah Smith Eccles, Naomi Minkoff, Corrina "Bubbles" Walton, Kim Logan, James Davis, Julie Ros, Bea Cassou, Cheri Hicks, Johnny Falls, Valerie Gebbia, Myron Witherell, Andrea and Peter Scheyhing, Ulrich, Ingrid, and Hugo Villbois, Jeffrey Furman, Emily Church, Chris Sulavik, Susan McGinnis, Carol Leff, Joseph and Kim Plaskett, Emile Molin, Tracy Toon, Jackie Prete, Martijn Dykstra, the Meinema family, Judy Agism, Bonnie Pressman, Alice Harris, Rico Williams, Aaron Martin, Susi Lux-Frayne, Marc-Henri Caillard, and Mark Herman: Thank you for teaching me what saying the words "I believe in you" and really meaning them can do for someone.

To Bankie Banx and Candy: Thank you for teaching me that being there for someone in the way that they need, no questions asked, is how you truly help someone unleash their potential.

To the Counter Canter Club: Thank you for teaching me what it means to drop everything and step into someone's life... all inspired by the love of an animal. Your Perfect Tyming is never forgotten!

To Debra Englander and everyone at Wiley: Thank you for teaching me that believing in someone and giving them a chance are the most important gifts you can give. The confidence you showed in my writing was one of the highlights of my career!

To Paul Fedorko: Thank you for teaching me about "positive perseverance."

To my Aunt Billie, Mason, Uncle Jr., Pooh, Leticia, Bobby, Minnie, Stanley, Reesa, Aunt Loyce, Maisa, Preston, Lourdes, Camilla, Alana, Imani, Uncle Jeffrey, Deborah, Veronica, Donald, Lil' Donald, Ashley, Mary Jane, Tex, Mr. Spratley, Tiger, and all of my family: Thank you for teaching me that family is the true "holy grail."

To the city of Bridgeport, Connecticut, especially ABCD, Longfellow School, and Messiah Baptist Church: Thank you for teaching me what it means for a community to truly be supportive of a family.

To all of the experts in this book who so selflessly gave their time and their wisdom to make this possible: Thank you for teaching me so much about human nature. Special thanks to Rick

Kahler and George Kinder, for their patience over the last few years, as I learned how much more there is to money than dollars and cents!

And to the brilliant Paula Boyer Kennedy: Thank you not only for being a great teacher, but for climbing out on that limb with me!

Paula Boyer Kennedy

To my husband, Joe Kennedy, and the kids, Carly and John Porciello, Dana and Nick Sorvillo, and Courtney Kennedy: Your common sense, humor, and wisdom keep my feet firmly planted on the ground.

To all my family: You know me well and love me anyway.

To my coauthor, Stacey Tisdale: You have enough energy for both of us.

To Bob Veres, editor of *Inside Information*: You introduced me to the best and the brightest.

To the financial planning community known as The Nazrudin Project: You inspire me.

To my colleagues and clients at Cammack LaRhette Consulting: You make it fun to go to work every day.

To my schoolmates at the Baldwin School, my sorority sisters at Delta Delta Delta (Cornell University), and my "grown-up" friends: You cheer me on.

To Paul Fedorko: You were a great encouragement.

To Debra Englander at Wiley: You kept asking me when I was going to write another book. Here it is, Debra.

Preface

First, Paula and I would like to thank you for buying *The True Cost of Happiness*. We realize you had many options. I recently did a search on Amazon.com for "personal finance" books, and there were 13,671 choices!

In addition, many of us associate the word "cost" with money. I wasn't quite sure how people would react to a book whose title could imply that "happiness" is something that can be bought with dollars and cents. Happiness does have a cost, but as you'll see in this book, it has little to do with money. You will also see, however, how your financial resources, whatever they may be, can play a role in creating a lifestyle that brings you happiness and peace.

Before I explain, let me tell you how this book came about. In the late 1990s I started working at CBS MarketWatch. This came after approximately seven years at the TV arm of *The Wall Street Journal*. The move to CBS MarketWatch took the focus of my reporting from Wall Street to Main Street. That's when I really started to learn about the "people side" of money. That's when I began to realize the contribution I wanted to make with my journalism—showing people how money can help them live better lives.

At CBS, I was able to do stories on everything from the latest guy who got rich on technology stocks, to the groups that were unable to participate in the wealth the markets were creating due primarily to socioeconomic circumstances. I also did a lot of personal finance reports, "How to get out of credit card debt," "Investing 101," "Finding personal finance advice that really works for you," and one my personal favorites, "What our financial choices tell us about our personalities . . . A look at what the financial choices of the people running for President of the United States say about who they really are."

I was always struck by the contradictions in my reporting. I could tell people the latest advice on responsible credit card use (I think even then there were about 13,671 pieces of advice out there), but in the same report I'd be saying the average household is racking up record amounts of credit card debt, while people are making more money than ever. Something wasn't adding up.

Move the clock forward a few years and I was reporting for CNN. I always wanted to use my journalism to raise awareness of the struggles of people in Africa, so in addition to my business reports, I jumped at the chance to report for a show called *Inside Africa* on CNN International.

Ultimately, many stories about Africa turned out to be stories about hope. To see how much people can accomplish with such limited financial resources is something everyone should witness. It is the ultimate reminder that real wealth has nothing to do with accumulating cash.

We all know this intellectually, but the struggles monetarily wealthy people have with money—despite their best efforts to stick to a budget or financial plan—and the unhappiness these struggles bring, are also very real.

I've heard and said many statements like:

- "If I had more money, I could spend more time doing the things that make me really happy."
- "If I had more money, I could be a better parent, because I'd have more time to spend with my children."
- "If I had more money, I wouldn't have to take on so much debt."

People sure blame an awful lot on money! It became clear that there was a lot of "stuff" behind our financial choices, and the journalist in me had to know what that "stuff" was and share the *Real Story*.

About four years ago, that quest led me to something called Life Planning. Life Planning is an integrated approach to financial management in which a person's beliefs, feelings, and thoughts about money are the jump-off point for the actual financial planning, versus just looking at the numbers side of the equation.

If you want to read more about what this methodology can do for your life, read Wynona Judd's book *Coming Home to Myself* (New York: New American Library, 2005), in which she talks about what Life Planner Rick Kahler, my friend and mentor, and his guidance have done for her life.

Life Planning appealed to my sense of logic because even I could see that it was not money that was causing the unhappiness or happiness that I witnessed, but the thoughts, beliefs, and feelings about money, and how they were playing out in people's behavior.

There is some controversy over the term *Life Planning*. Some people in the financial world argue that getting to know what's driving someone's financial choices is just good financial planning. It was my observation, however, that the planners who take this integrated approach had or incorporated a different set of skills into their practices—the kinds of skills needed to help people tease apart their thoughts and beliefs.

As you'll see, the factors behind our financial choices run very deep. They are rooted in our childhoods, social messages, and the ways in which we perceive ourselves. I have seen countless numbers of people try to change their behavior without addressing the root causes, only to end up exactly where they started.

Looking at the "why" behind our financial choices is the only way we can bridge that gap between what we know and what we do. It is taking a look at that space—that gap where change and choice reside—that will reveal the answers I believe you are looking for. I've observed time and time again that some understanding of what's behind our actions is imperative if lasting change is to occur.

So I thought I had the story I was looking for, and off I went to write a book about Life Planning. I would show John Doe that his debt is largely rooted in the "I'm going to have a big pay-off one day" message he got from his father. I would show Jane Doe that social messages about men making big financial decisions were behind her belief that she didn't know how to manage money. I would show Jack Doe how social messages that his ethnic group is a bad financial risk were becoming a self-fulfilling prophecy in his own life. The lists go on and on.

I spent about two years thinking I had the whole story. I worked on book proposals and marketing plans, and was rejected by publisher after publisher. Then a series of personal events happened that changed my life so profoundly, I was left with no choice but to deepen my examination of the nature of happiness, unhappiness, and change.

Within 11 months, the two most important women in my life passed, and I gave birth to Christopher. To lose your mother, three weeks later unexpectedly lose your grandmother, four weeks later find out you're pregnant, and nine months later give birth to a child unleashes "everything all at once," as I'm fond of saying. You have no choice but to sit back, hold on, and watch.

What I saw was the miracle of human nature. If someone had told me that the deep feelings of grief I experienced could give way to the happiness that I feel today, I would have found that very hard to believe. The truth is, I cried, but I stopped crying. I hurt, but I stopped hurting, all without lifting a finger. My actions and behaviors changed from those of someone who was in enormous pain and grieving to those of a woman whose life was now empowered with the boundless and joyful energy that comes with motherhood.

What I saw was that we are built with everything we need to transform unhappiness and discontent into happiness. It is a process that takes place on the inside and is unaffected by external actions or circumstances.

What I saw was that all the people I had met and interviewed were looking outside of themselves, in this instance, to money to cure their unhappiness and discontent, when all money was actually doing was making them forget what they are truly capable of—change and transformation on a visceral level. If something as profound of grief can change, the feelings and beliefs that drive our financial choices can be transformed as well.

This book then became about looking at that place where transformation occurs and giving you the tools to create an environment that makes it possible. I not only had the story I was really looking for, but soon found a publisher who wanted to tell it!

As I moved forward, someone kept coming to mind whom I had interviewed in my previous research of Life Planning, Paula Boyer Kennedy. Her ability to make this integrated financial approach so simple and approachable had always caught my attention. Paula and I continued to talk about Life Planning, and then decided to collaborate.

As you will see, in Part II of this book, her financial planning skills and deep understanding of human nature—and the effects that money can have on it—will truly give you the skills to use your financial choices to help make the grandest statement of who you really are.

Paula and I feel that an integrated approach to financial planning is more important than ever. We are living longer, more productive lives than any generations in history. Baby Boomers are shattering our old notions of what it means to retire. Some are starting new careers. Some are going out into the world and trying to make a difference, instead of settling into the tranquility and peace they may have imagined for this time in their lives.

Many members of Generation X are just starting families as they approach and pass their 40th year. Many are taking the time, and giving themselves the experiences needed to figure out what they really want to be when they grow up.

Yet these generations face:

- The highest health care bills in history for themselves and their parents.
- The need to use assets meant to be inherited by their children to pay for things like retirement and eldercare.
- Disappearing corporate retirement benefits.

This all comes at a time when families and individuals are carrying historically high debt and historically low savings. We can no longer afford this given the reality of our longer lives. The money simply won't last. We can no longer afford financial illiteracy for ourselves and our children.

In addition to the age/money equation, our attitudes have changed. Quality of life has taken on a new meaning in the post-9/11 world. The things we value have changed. More men and women are walking away from high-paying jobs to spend more time with their families. In this post-Enron world, spending without accountability is no longer the accepted norm. We want to know what corporate officers are doing with our investment dollars. We want to know that corporations and nations are not cutting corners that hurt our environment in order to make money. We are giving more money to charities than ever before. These are our new realities.

We applaud you for taking responsibility for your finances and your happiness. We wish you all the luck in the world as you embark on this journey!

PART I

A LOOK INSIDE

CHAPTER 1

Working Together

If you and I were sitting at Starbucks discussing the things you want to accomplish in your life, and how your financial situation is playing into that equation, I would start gushing about a form of financial management called Life Planning.

I would tell you how this is the only form of financial planning that I've seen bring lasting results to people. I'd also tell you that the reason I think it works so well is that it helps people figure out *why* they make the decisions they do about making and spending money.

I would also probably say something like, "Telling someone to stop overspending without taking a look at *why* they're doing it in the first place is like telling someone to go on a fad diet without looking at what's driving the overeating. They may be able to change their behavior for a time, but sooner or later, the reasons behind it will regain control of their actions."

After we discussed the merits of that logic, I'm sure I would start explaining "The Big Three." Those are the three major influences behind our choices about making and spending money:

The Big Three

1. The lessons we learned about money when we were growing up
2. The messages society tells us about money
3. The messages we tell ourselves about money

At this point, I would shift into reporter mode and start asking you the most effective questions I've seen Life Planners use to help them

3

discover the influence The Big Three are having on their clients, so that we could see how those factors are affecting your financial choices.

The Questions

One of the things that first caught my eye about Life Planning was the difference in the questions these planners ask their clients versus those asked by traditional financial planners.

These are a few questions from a questionnaire I once saw used by a major brokerage house to help identify their client's needs:

- How much money do you think you will need to live when you retire?
- Where do you want your finances to be in 5 years?
- Where do you want your finances to be in 10 years?

These are some of the questions that Life Planners ask:

- In what era did your primary caregiver grow up?
- How did the attitudes of their generation play into what they taught you about money? Do those teachings serve you today?
- If you found out you had five years to live, how would you change your life?

Every reporter knows that the best way to uncover relevant information is by asking the *right* questions. I think you can see the difference in the level of knowledge these different methods seek.

Back at Starbucks …

After we'd talked about some questions that would help you see how The Big Three have influenced your choices about making and spending money, you would have some great insights, and consequently more options, for dealing with some of the barriers that may be blocking you from the life you really want.

Whether you choose to break down those barriers, step over them, or deal with them at another time, I would urge you to move forward and create the financial plan to support that life.

Next, I would direct you to one of the amazing professionals I've met through my study of Life Planning, so that they could help you make the financial choices that would allow you to reach your goals.

In reality, we're not sitting together in Starbucks having this discussion, but with your help, I can show you how to create a lifestyle that reflects who you really are. In addition, with the help of Paula Kennedy, one of the most effective planners in the United States, you will learn how to use your finances to support that journey.

> ### Pearls from Planners
>
> In my effort to give you access to the professionals who can help make your goals a reality, I have included some of their advice in sidebars like this one called "Pearls from Planners." They consist primarily of excerpts from interviews I've conducted with the experts I feel are the best in the business of helping people practice mindful money management. These pearls of wisdom will help clarify and explain this process for you.

No Shortcuts

There's no way around it. Reallocating your finances so that they support your most important goals and priorities requires putting some pen to paper (or finger to keyboard).

Throughout this process you will be clarifying your goals, reflecting on some of your attitudes and beliefs about money, and creating an actual financial blueprint to guide you in your quest to make your dream life a reality.

There will be spaces for writing in the book, but you may want to get a notebook or designate a computer file for the exercises.

You as the Reporter

Despite their sometimes controversial outcomes, reporters commit themselves to getting to the truth of a matter. In Part I of this book, I'm going to ask you to play reporter so that we get the real story on how The Big Three have influenced your financial life.

The idea of this exercise is to get you to look at these aspects of your life from the perspective of an *observer*. It's not your job to judge or spin the story. We simply want to tap into your objectivity, so that we can present as truthful account as possible of the ways in which your family, society, and the messages you tell yourself about money have impacted your financial choices.

In order to help you do this, I will give you a series of questions in the following chapters that will essentially allow you to interview yourself. At each chapter's conclusion, you will get an outline that will allow you to construct a *report* we'll call "Your Story," on each of these aspects of your life.

We use these stories so that you have a concise point of reference when Paula helps you literally account for what The Big Three are costing you, in Part II of this book.

So, let's have fun with these exercises! It's just you, me, and Paula. There's no reason to hold back.

The Interview Zone

I'm sure you've heard the phrase "in the zone." It generally refers to a deep state of concentration when it almost feels like time is standing still. Nothing exists except you and your task at hand. People generally do their best work when they're in this mode.

"The zone" is a place of complete honesty, without distraction from outside thoughts or influences. That's how we're trying to see you, undistracted by influences from The Big Three.

One of my favorite parts of being a reporter is going into what I call "The Interview Zone." In most instances, when you sit down to interview someone, a stillness and honesty take hold of the environment that is hard to put into words. Think about the last time you had a real heart-to-heart conversation with someone, and you just *knew* that they were telling the truth. It feels a bit like that.

A good interviewer tries to achieve this each time they sit down with someone (unless, of course, we're talking about an unwilling subject).

I asked arguably the greatest interviewer of all time to help me put this into words for you. CBS *60 Minutes* news legend Mike Wallace explained it to me like this:

> When someone realizes that you have put in the time to read
> and do your research about them before you sit down, they
> come to respect the time and care that you have taken with their
> story. This creates what I call a "chemistry of confidentiality."
> When you look a person in the eye, and they realize, "Hey, this
> guy cares about my story," they want to open up.

We will do the research and put in the time and care that's necessary to create an environment that allows you to open up. We will create the "chemistry of confidentiality" Mike describes as you examine the questions in the following chapters. Don't hold back—this information is confidential.

CHAPTER 2

A Little Awareness Goes a Long Way

Believe it or not, one of the most insightful discussions I've had about what makes Life Planning work was with Sally Kempton, meditation master and author of *The Heart of Meditation* (South Fallsburg, N.Y.: Siddha Yoga Publications, 2002).

The conversation came about because I was trying to get a clear answer of why the term *awareness* kept coming up in all of my discussions about the difference between Life Planning and traditional financial management. I would grill planners about why people are able to make such swift and lasting changes to their lives when they undertake this process. Time and time again, I would hear that it's the awareness of the issues behind their behavior that makes the difference. I turned to Ms. Kempton because the term *awareness* also consistently came up when I was doing research on different spiritual practices.

Part of the emphasis on awareness as a key component to financial planning made sense to me. Even I know that the first step in making any change is becoming *aware* that a change needs to be made. So why doesn't the awareness that smoking is bad for us make everybody quit? Why doesn't the awareness that obesity kills make everybody lose weight? What about awareness that credit card debt is akin to wearing cement shoes in the ocean when it comes to productive financial behavior?

Awareness alone was clearly not the answer, yet I knew this was the heart of the story. If I could define that magic moment where insight turns to action, I could help you find success on many levels. I interviewed planners, people who'd undergone transformations, psychologists, psychiatrists, spiritual advisers like Ms. Kempton, everyone I could think of. Still, I wasn't getting that, "Here's how it works!" answer I was looking for:

Awareness + ? = Successful Financial Management

The reason my discussion with Ms. Kempton was so enlightening is that she helped me realize that I was trying to define awareness as a *thing* that could be thrown into a formula, when in reality it is a *place* we each arrive at in our own time.

"The kind of heart-piercing awareness that brings about change is a glimpse of the truth itself. Truth has power that is strong enough to transform us."

Awareness is not a thing, but the place where that transformation occurs.

"It's that space where we have that intuitive flash of 'I have to stop doing this!' That life-changing, no-turning-back moment. You can't get there until you get there," Ms. Kempton told me during our interview.

Pearls from Planners

Once that light bulb comes on, for many people, the change is instant. We want to do the right thing, we want to do the good thing, and in many instances, we have no idea that what we're doing is self-destructive and self-defeating. We may even be victimizing our children by our behavior! Still, you have to be willing to walk in the doorway and begin looking, to see what's there. What makes people willing to do this is usually some pain related to their money behavior. It could be losing a company, or a home, fighting with a spouse, etc., but there is usually a catalyst behind a true willingness to change behavior.

Dr. Ted Klontz, PhD psychology, specializing in financial behavior; contributing author, *Chicken Soup for the Recovering Soul*; CEO onsite workshops

And If "Awareness" Alone Doesn't Work . . .

Awareness, and the "aha" flashes of insight it brings, is enough for some people to change their behavior.

That can leave the rest of us feeling like we are in someway deficient. How come I don't save more and invest more, even though I'm *aware* that it would bring me closer to my goals? What's wrong with me?

I interviewed Dr. James Prochaska, coauthor of *Changing for Good* (New York: William Morrow, 1994), about this topic. (You'll hear a lot more about him in Chapter 9, when we look at successful processes for change.)

He pointed out that one of the major reasons so many of us have these paralyzing feelings of deficiency is that, historically, we're given two choices when it comes to claiming that we've been successful at making changes: action or inaction. For example, think of all of the New Year's resolutions out there to spend less or stop going into credit card debt.

As soon as we break the resolution, many of us allow an "I'm a failure" cloud to hover over many of the ways in which we perceive ourselves.

Dr. Prochaska points out that just because the New Year is here and you are not prepared to make those changes doesn't mean that you aren't well on your way to the transformation you desire. He challenges us to think of change in terms of *progression*, instead of the all-or-nothing way in which we are programmed to think.

You have already started down the road of aligning your finances with your priorities or you wouldn't be reading this book. Do not make change contingent on some big cosmic shift in your thinking or who you are. You're just fine. You got yourself to this point, this page, and this process. Your level of awareness has already brought you to that place where transformation can occur!

3

The Big Picture

WHAT YOU'RE PLANNING FOR

I always marvel at the ways in which most of us stumble when we try and verbalize what we want to do with our lives. We have ideas: "Spend quality time with family," "See the world," "Make a difference," but the ideas are usually short on specifics. Rarely do we have a plan to live out those goals as soon as we would like to.

This isn't a dress rehearsal—this is your real life! This is your one chance to do the things you care about.

Seeing that *big picture*—those things we want to achieve—is challenging, especially when we are so focused on our day-to-day lives.

It becomes easy to forget that our dreams are worth accomplishing. In fact, the things we dream about are clues to where our true happiness lies.

Let's clarify your goals and dreams so that we can create a financial plan to support them.

Thinking about What's Important

The most effective exercise I have seen in helping people clarify their goals was created by George Kinder, author of *The Seven Stages of Money Maturity* (New York: Dell, 2000). George is recognized as the founder of the Life Planning movement. *Financial Planning* magazine, the gold standard when it comes to publications for the industry, has named him as one of the six "most influential" financial planners in America. The other five have all studied with him! At his Kinder Institute of Life Planning, planners from all over the world learn how to apply Life Planning techniques in their work with their clients.

In his exercises, George has people think about three scenarios. He's been generous enough to allow me to share them with you.

The first one is called "Plenty of Money." You have all of the money you will ever need, now or in the future. You may not be Aristotle Onassis rich, but money will never again be a concern. What will you do with it? From this moment forward, what will you do with your life? Your time?

Pearls from Planners

As you write your answer, it's important to let yourself dream when you consider this scenario. It's very revealing. "Give yourself the right to have, do, or be, anything that comes to mind." This exercise has nothing to do with realism.

George Kinder

Write down what your "Plenty of Money" life looks like, before you move on to the next scenario. (*Note:* Parents, please try and give some consideration to this scenario that does not involve your children.)

_____

_____

_____

_____

_____

In the second scenario, you've just come from the doctor, and you find out you only have 5 to 10 years to live. Your disease will not cause you physical discomfort. Your death will be sudden and unpredictable. Knowing death is coming sooner than you expected, how will you change your life? What will you do in the time you have remaining?

Pearls from Planners

While the "Plenty of Money" scenario may reveal material desires like a bigger house or exotic vacations, the "Just a Few Years Left" scenario removes some of the material trappings. It also uncovers areas of vulnerability and reveals parts of our lives that need to be resolved, not swept under the rug. Let the emotional import of the situation really sink in!

George Kinder

What would your life look like if you only had 5 to 10 years left?

_____

_____

_____

_____

_____

In the third and final scenario, you've gone to the doctor and found out you'll be dead within 24 hours. The question is *not* what you would do with the time you have left, but what are your regrets? What are your longings and feelings? What are your deep and un- fulfilled dreams? What do you wish you had accomplished in this precious life that is just about to end?

Use your imagination to put yourself into this final scenario. Write down your thoughts and reflections.

_____

_____

_____

_____

_____

Pearls from Planners

"Twenty-four Hours to Go" cuts deepest of all. It becomes clear which issues in life are superficial and which are central. Sometimes this exercise delivers a major surprise. A longing or a wish that has never before surfaced ... Not simply to a financial adviser, but often to oneself.

George Kinder

George once had a client who wanted advice about handling her retirement accounts. He took her through the three scenarios. In the first, "Plenty of Money," she discovered that she wanted to become self-employed so that she would have more flexibility in her life. If money was not a concern, she would have homes on the Atlantic and Pacific coasts, write a book, and do some public speaking.

The "Just a Few Years Left," scenario revealed a desire on her part to spend more time with her niece, as well as going to Nepal to see Mount Everest.

With just "Twenty-four Hours to Go," this woman regretted that she'd never learned how to speak with more authority, which was connected to her dream of public speaking in the first scenario. Another big regret was not meeting the love of her life.

George helped her align her financial resources and her true priorities. He helped her downsize her life and get rid of assets that were a drain on the resources she had for the things she really wanted to do. That freed up money to prepare for self-employment and a bicoastal existence in retirement.

In addition, they cut spending on things that were not high on her priority list. That freed up money to take courses that would help her strengthen her communication skills.

Once this woman began to channel her resources toward her goals, channeling her time toward her priorities began to happen naturally. She began to put herself in positions where she could meet someone with whom she might develop a long-term relationship, perhaps someone who also wanted to make that trek to Everest! She also made time to spend with her niece, and eventually write that book.

Your Goals

Think about what you've learned about yourself as you imagined these different scenarios. What did you learn about your priorities? What did you learn about your goals in the following five areas?

1. What are your *personal goals*? What *experiences* would you like to have during your lifetime? George's client, for example, wanted to write a book and go to Nepal.

   _____

   _____

   _____

   _____

   _____

2. What goals do you have for your *family*? Perhaps living in a certain part of the world for a while or sending your children to a certain school?

   _____

   _____

   _____

   _____

   _____

3. Did you discover any *big picture*, or *worldly* goals, like giving money to a charity, or helping someone who needs emotional or financial support?

   _____

   _____

   _____

   _____

   _____

4. Think about your goals when it comes to the *legacy* you want to leave behind. Allocating some of your wealth to a cause that's important to you, for example, or making sure your

family doesn't bear any financial burdens because of decisions you've made.

_____

_____

_____

_____

_____

5. What are some of the *material* goals you've discovered? George's client, for example, learned that she wanted to have residences on the Atlantic and Pacific coasts.

_____

_____

_____

_____

_____

Let's move forward and identify any beliefs and behaviors that may be keeping you from honoring these goals.

CHAPTER 4

The Price of Pleasing
Mom and Pop

ARE YOUR EARLY LESSONS WORKING
FOR YOU OR AGAINST YOU?

I think one of the most surprising things I discovered as I delved into Life Planning was how big a role our family dynamics, or early "money scripts," as many planners and psychologists call them, play in our financial behavior.

When I say family dynamic, I do not mean the trials and tribulations of trying to live in financial harmony with a spouse or partner—that gets is own chapter. I'm talking about the ways in which the first lessons we learned about money as children affect our decisions about making and spending it as adults.

Pearls from Planners

"If you think of an unconscious belief as a script, it's easy to understand it as a set of instructions written by someone else. Actors are given scripts, which they rehearse until they can follow them perfectly. In the same way, we blindly follow our money scripts. We've learned our parts well, and we faithfully act them out."

Rick Kahler, President, Kahler Financial Group; coauthor, *Conscious Finance* (Rapid City, S.D.: FoxCraft, 2005) and *The Financial Wisdom of Ebenezer Scrooge* (Deerfield Beach, Fla.: HCI, 2005)

Psychobabble?

Initially, the notion that our adult financial behavior was rooted in our childhoods sounded like it could be a bit of psychobabble. The cynic in me thought that the "blame it on mom and dad" rationale would work as a great excuse for people who want to justify irrational financial behavior. Still . . .

All beliefs, attitudes, and, consequently, behavior come from somewhere.

Planners across the board say that *somewhere*, when it comes to money, lies largely in our childhoods.

Pearls from Planners

"We simply filter information through the mechanisms we developed as a child. Those deep imprints influence every decision we make, and we use them as a reference point. If we don't go back and look at those operating systems, we will fail. We will remain at that level of understanding if it is not revisited."

Susan Galvan, cofounder, The Kinder Institute of Life Planning

Money Scripts at Work

When I took this information into the field and started examining the family dynamic at work in ordinary people, it was easy to see those early money scripts at work.

A planner told me about a client who decided to seek professional help because she and her husband were having a hard time talking about money and integrating their finances. In fact, they'd always filed separate tax returns. The first thing the planner asked them to do was to fully disclose all of their assets.

This woman very reluctantly gave the planner her financial statements. She was a lawyer and her husband an artist. They both knew she made more money, but she kept much of her earnings a secret.

When her husband saw how much money she really made, he felt hurt and angry. He saw her choice to hide her financial worth from him as a sign of distrust.

This woman still felt very justified in her actions. She truly believed that secrecy was the only way to avoid unpleasant discussions about money.

Their planner, a professionally trained therapist who focuses on financial issues, started asking questions about how this couple saw their parents behave with money.

It turns out that this woman's father would always yell at her mother about her spending. In order to avoid these brutal confrontations, her mother would buy things and not tell her father. She and her daughter would go clothes shopping, for example, and show the father only some of the purchases. The mother would incorporate the daughter's help in hiding many of the items they bought.

The child just fell into the "hide money" mode as an adult, unaware of the trouble the secrecy was bringing to her marriage.

We're going to:

- Spotlight some of your parents' or primary caregivers' beliefs about money.
- See how those beliefs are playing into your financial behavior.
- Identify early experiences with money that have left an impression.

Once you become aware of these influences, you will have a greater understanding of some of your own financial tendencies and habits. The information will help you determine if some of those early scripts need to be rewritten in order to help you make better choices—choices that bring you closer to your goals and priorities.

Where They Were Coming From

- Your father's belief that life begins when you retire.
- Your mother's decision to let the "man of the house" handle all of the finances.
- The ever-so-popular "Don't talk about money in front of the children."

Chances are, when you were growing up, you didn't have the presence of mind to say:

- "Dad, I don't want to put off my best days until I'm 65."
- "Mom, you're teaching me to give away a lot of my personal power."
- "Mom and Dad, is it really best to avoid challenging subjects?"

Chances are also that your primary caregivers didn't realize that their unspoken words were speaking volumes! Still, I'm going to go out on a limb and assume that they did not intentionally give you messages about money that may not serve your best interests.

Pearls from Planners

"This conversation is not about blaming mom and dad. It's really about discovering the messages that you got, some recognizable, and some unspoken, that have formed you now. If they're good, you want to keep them. If not, instead of blaming mom and dad, see what you can do differently."

Marty Carter, family counselor specializing in financial behavior; licensed clinical social worker

It's important to remember that the person or people who raised you were working from their own money scripts, which were created in very different times. If they grew up during the Great Depression or the financial chaos that came in its wake, for example, they may carry a lot of fear that money will run out, even if it's not a financial reality. The questions become: How did that fear manifest in the example they were setting for you? How is it playing out in your behavior today?

In order to get *your story*, we need an idea of where they were coming from.

Think about the following questions. Take notes in the book, in your notebook, or on your computer. We'll need to refer to this information at the end of this chapter.

- What were your primary caregivers' financial circumstances when they grew up? Was money, or the lack thereof, a big factor in their childhood? What impact do you think this had on their financial beliefs and behaviors?
- In what era did they grow up (the Depression, the 1960s, etc.)? Do you think this had an impact on their financial attitudes as adults?
- What were the social attitudes regarding money during that time? Were there fears that there was not enough to go

around? A make love, not war, or money sentiment? Do you think they adopted these attitudes in their own values?
- What kind of role-playing do you think they saw when it came to financial management? For example, did their father manage the money while their mother stayed out of the finances? Did the opposite happen?
- What was your primary caregivers' prevailing attitude about money? Were your parents spenders, savers, debtors, etc.?

Think about your parents, or primary caregivers as children. Write a few sentences about how their childhood experiences formed their adult attitudes and behaviors. This exercise will give you helpful insights into your own story.

_____

_____

_____

_____

_____

First Impressions

Perhaps when you think about the experiences the person or people who raised you had with money, it's easier to understand the lessons they taught you.

The following questions will help you identify the scripts from which you've been working:

- Who managed the money in your household? What role did their spouse or partner play? Do you see this dynamic playing out in your financial life? What do you think of this?
- Were your primary caregivers secretive or open about the family finances? Do you see this in your own behavior? What do you think of this?
- Was there stress around money in your household? How has that affected you today?
- How did your family interact or fight about money? (Many planners say all families fight about money, even if it's not verbal.) Do you see this at play in your own behavior?

- What did your primary caregivers emphasize to you as the most important thing to know about money, not only by their words, but by their actions? How is that affecting you today?
- What were the attitudes about saving, debt, investing, insurance, and charity in your household?
- When you look at your parents' or caregivers' attitudes and actions about retirement planning, what do you think they taught you about this time of your life? What do you think of these lessons?
- Do you think "keeping up with the Joneses" (having an equal lifestyle and possessions compared to those around them) was important to your primary caregivers? What do you think of this?
- Did your primary caregivers ever tell you how you should earn money (e.g., "You should be a doctor"), or were they more likely to encourage you to find and follow your passions? How has this affected you today?
- Did your family have debt aside from a mortgage? What was their attitude toward it? Do you see that playing out in your attitudes and behaviors regarding debt?
- What did you admire the most about your primary caregivers' financial behavior? Why?
- What do you consider to be your primary caregiver(s)' greatest limitations when it comes to money? How do you think it affected them? What do you think of this?
- If there was more than one child in your household, did your primary caregivers treat you all the same when it came to money? If not, how was it different? What do you think of this?
- Imagine yourself achieving your goals. What would you be doing differently with your finances? Which of your early money scripts would have to be reexamined?

These questions are a lot to think about, but the answers paint a very good picture of the early scripting you were given about money. Use the answers to write a summary of what the child you once were saw when it came to their parents' or primary caregivers' relationship with money. Give special attention to the questions that really strike a nerve. Many of the planners and therapists I've interviewed say that's likely where much of the "emotional pay dirt" is hiding.

_____

_____

_____

_____

_____

Other Imprints

You should be getting an idea of where some of your current beliefs and behaviors surrounding money came from. While many come from your primary caregivers, planners also say there may have been outside experiences that left a big impression.

This certainly isn't my most pleasant childhood memory, but perhaps it will help you understand what they mean.

As I child, I was often teased by a few bullies for being the only black person in school. I never told my parents; I didn't want to upset them, and didn't see much point, because I felt that I was in a circumstance that was not going to change. I did notice, however, that the bullies stopped teasing me when I gave them things. So, I began to take money out of a jar of coins my mother kept next to her bed, and use them in the vending machines at school. I would buy the bullies candy, soda, cookies at school bake sales—anything to _buy_ brief respites from the teasing.

I use this as an example, because when I think back to experiences with money that have stayed with me, it's still in my thoughts. It clearly left an impression! It's up to me to make sure that the "resolve conflicts with gifts" message this experience could teach does not creep up in my adult behavior.

Do you have childhood memories of any experiences with money that just won't disappear? Tell me about them. It could be a circumstance like mine. It could be an event, a person—anything that left an impression that has stayed with you.

_____

_____

_____

_____

_____

Your Story

We've shaken up quite a bit of information about your first impressions about money. We're going to consolidate it into an outline we'll call "Your Story," as I mentioned in Chapter 1. This story, and those that you create in the following chapters, will serve as concise points of reference, as you create a financial plan in Part II.

You will need to consider things like your childhood lessons in your financial planning. You'll want to build on behaviors and attitudes that bring you closer to your goals. You can make different choices when you realize that some of your early impressions may be driving behaviors that don't serve your best interests.

Really have fun with this exercise! Think of it as an in-depth report about a very important person—you. The hot news anchor du jour will be reading it on the evening news. The good news is that you are also the only member of the audience, so you don't have to hold back.

Creating a story in the third person like this is a wonderful way to put yourself in an objective, witnessing state of mind. This exercise—and this book, for that matter—is not about playing judge and jury. It's not about criticizing or critiquing your financial beliefs and behaviors; we simply want to identify them.

You'll notice when you get to the outline for "Your Story" that I use the word *parents* when I refer to your primary caregivers. Not all of us were raised by our parents. This was done for ease of production. Please make any necessary adjustments on my behalf.

John's First Lessons About Money—Are They Helping Him Now?

Here is a completed outline. It can serve as a guide when you create "Your Story."

In tonight's broadcast: A look at the ways in which the financial lessons we learned from our parents affect the choices we make as adults.

When **John** was growing up, his parents taught him the following lessons about money:

- Managing money was the **man's job** in the household.
- Children **should not be involved** in discussions about money.
- Saving money is **the most important thing you can do**.

- Debt **was a way to help make ends meet**, and investing was **for the rich**.
- When it came to planning for the future and retirement, John's parents **did not prepare for** this part of their lives.

John understands why his parents taught him the lessons they did. When they grew up, **there was a scarcity of money** in their family. They were also raised in the **Depression era**, when the prevailing attitude about money was **a fear that there was not enough to go around**.

While John admires what his parent's taught him about **saving**, he does not think their lessons about **debt, investing, retirement planning**, and **communication**, serve him well today.

He sees those lessons playing out in his behavior in the following ways:

- All of his credit cards are maxed out.
- He's always been afraid to invest in stocks.
- He only has a few thousand dollars in his retirement account.
- He does not talk to his kids about money.

In addition to the lessons he learned from his parents, **the fact that his brother always stole his money** left a big impression on John's behavior. He notices this play out the following way: **He doesn't trust anyone when it comes to helping him make financial decisions**.

In order for John to achieve his goals, despite some of those early lessons, he knows he must take the following actions:

- Come up with a plan to pay off his credit card debt.
- Grow his savings through investing.
- Learn how to trust financial advisers.
- Start planning and saving for the store he wants to open when he retires.
- Teach his kids how to manage money.

We here at the station applaud John in his efforts to make the life he wants become a reality!

A Look at How the Financial Lessons We Learned from Our Parents Affect the Choices We Make as Adults

Again, use John's story as a guide if you have any questions.

When *(your name)* was growing up, *his/her* parent(s) taught *him/her* the following lessons about money:

- Managing money was _____ job in the household.
- Children_____ in discussions about money.
- Saving money is _____.
- Debt is _____, and investing is _____.
- When it came to planning for the future and retirement, *(your name's)* parents_____ for this part of their lives.

(Your name) understands why *his/her* parents taught *him/her* the lessons they did. When they grew up, money _____ _____in their family. They were also raised in the _____ era, when the prevailing attitude about money was _____ _____.

While *(your name)* admires what *his/her* parents taught *him/her* about _____ _____, *he/she* does not think their lessons about _____ _____ _____ _____ _____ serve *him/her* well today.

He/she sees those lessons playing out in his/her behavior in the following ways:

_____ _____ _____

_____

_____

In addition to the lessons _he/she_ learned from _his/her_ parents, _____left a big impression on _(your name's)_ behavior. _He/she_ notices this play out in the following ways:

_____

_____

_____

_____

In order for _(your name)_ to achieve _his/her_ goals, despite some of those early lessons, he knows _he/she_ must take the following actions:

_____

_____

_____

_____

We here at the station applaud _(your name)_ in _his/her_ efforts to make the life _he/she_ wants become a reality!

Moving Forward

In Chapter 9, we take a hard look at what it takes to make lasting change to your financial behavior. Until we get to there, however, take note of the specific ways in which your early money scripts are playing out in your choices. Let that little light bulb go off, for example, if you catch yourself making important financial decisions without consulting your spouse—just like dad.

In addition, think about some of the lessons your primary caregivers taught you that you want to build upon. For example, like John, you may be thankful for your lessons about saving money. Make sure you're honoring these lessons in your financial behavior. If not, try and do something to respect those teachings at least once a week. Put $10 in your savings account. Go for a walk instead of going shopping. Buy something on eBay instead of paying full retail price. Just do something each week to stay connected with those values.

Also, think about those money scripts that are limiting you. Imagine your life without those messages. How would your actions be different? How would your thoughts and reactions be different? How would your conversations be different?

Try putting what you've imagined into practice, walk the walk, and talk the talk, even if your scripts are still locked in. Adjust your thoughts, your actions, and the things you tell yourself and others. Cut up a credit card, if you find yourself falling into scripted debt patterns. Talk to your banker, accountant, friends, and family, about stocks, if you've been scripted to avoid the markets. Again, we talk more about what it takes to change behavior in Chapter 9. For the time being, do one of these exercises at least once a week. Notice how your experiences change.

CHAPTER 5

Social Messages

- A bond trader/mother leaves home at 5 A.M. and returns at 7 P.M., five days a week. She doesn't like her job or her hours, but her income is necessary to live in the "right" neighborhood, and send her children to the "right" schools.
- A widow is falling into financial chaos because she had no idea how the family finances worked after her husband died. She freely admits that she always viewed managing money as the man's job.
- An African-American woman has racked up thousands of dollars' worth of credit card debt, and justifies it by saying, "*We do what we have to.*" She's referring to her belief that social and economic disadvantages force African-Americans to take on debt in order to maintain a "normal" standard of living.

I interviewed these three women and many people like them, and they all have two things in common:

1. Their financial situations are making them miserable.
2. They are *unconsciously* doing exactly what societal messages tell them they should.

Whether it's the pressure to "keep up with the Joneses" or the messages society and the media send us about the ways certain gender and ethnic groups should behave, when it comes to money, societal scripts are one of the biggest influences on all of our financial behavior.

Life Planners make clients take a long, hard look at the impact social pressures have on their choices, acknowledging that it would be difficult, if not impossible, to align spending with priorities, without looking at the ways in which societal messages knock us off course.

Pearls from Planners

"The thing which many planners have not yet seized upon is that these large social and cultural boundaries, the context within which people live out their lives, are at least as important as the psychological traits individuals bring to financial decisions. Even more so, because they set the very parameters by which we live."

Daniel J. Monti, PhD, professor of sociology, Boston University; founder, InnerCity Entrepreneurs

---

Let's find out which social scripts are influencing your behavior and determine if those messages are allowing you to live in sync with who you really are.

In order to put together "Your Story," we'll look at:

- The messages you've received from "the Joneses"
- The scripts you might be following regarding your gender
- The scripts you might be following regarding your race and ethnic group

Food for Thought

Before we begin, there's something I would like for you to think about. When it comes to aligning financial choices with values, Lynne Twist's work is among the most respected.

Twist, author of *The Soul of Money* (New York: W. W. Norton, 2003), and founder of The Soul of Money Institute, has catalyzed much debate and thinking about this topic through what she has identified as "Three Myths of Scarcity." Planners say in one way or another, they are at the root of *all* financial behavior that is out of sync with our true natures.

I ask you to think about these myths before we look at societal messages because I see them deeply embedded in much of our social scripting.

Myth 1: There's Not Enough to Go Around

Planners say this myth fosters an "I've got to make sure that I get my share of the pie" mentality, which can justify all sorts of irrational behavior.

Myth 2: More Is Better

I'll have enough when I get more. This belief can put us on a never-ending treadmill that does not allow time to examine our priorities, let alone align our behavior with them.

Myth 3: That's Just the Way It Is

I think there's a disguise in this one. While it is full of hopelessness and resignation, in its root, the belief that there is nothing a person can do about his given circumstance is also a great ally when it comes to resisting change. "That's just how I am" is probably one of the most overused excuses in history, financial behavior being no exception!

Pearls from Planners

"If you really release the lies of scarcity, it frees up oceans of energy. When you let go of trying to get more of what you don't really need, it frees up enormous energy to make a difference with what you have. . . . When you try to hoard and hold onto money, out of fear, it becomes toxic to those holding it, and you lose your touch with the rest of the world, which is so important to stay humble, and stay in touch with who you are."

Lynne Twist

What are your thoughts on Twist's three myths? Do you see them at work in your own behavior? If so, how would your beliefs and actions change, if you were free from these myths?

_____

_____

_____

_____

_____

The Joneses Got Rich

Keeping up with the Joneses ain't what it used to be for one simple reason:

The Joneses got rich!

Or at least, they sure look like it! They've moved into McMansions with garages big enough to house their $30,000+ SUVs. Flat-screen TVs, fancy computers, and gadgets to listen to 30,000+ songs are now "necessity" items. The Joneses vacation in the most fashionable destinations and send their kids to expensive schools. They send them away for summers in Europe or to places with unpronounceable names. The Jones children are donning the same clothes their heroes—Britney, Paris, Beyonce, and Brangelina—are wearing on the evening entertainment shows.

In order to pay for their lifestyle, the Joneses—and those trying to keep up with them—have embraced about $8,000 in credit card debt—more than double the $3,000 they carried in 1990. They have also achieved a negative savings rate. In addition, they are working more hours than ever to pay for their standard of living.

When Harvard economist James Duesenberry popularized the phrase "keeping up with the Joneses" in 1952, it was part of a model he created to show how neighbors try to keep up with each other in terms of purchases, like dishwashers, second cars, televisions, and so on.

Many economists and sociologists feel that Duesenberry's family has worked so hard to create their high-end lifestyle that they've *earned* a new name. Many now use the phrase "keeping up with the Gateses" (yes, they mean Bill and Melinda), to illustrate the fact that "keeping up" in today's society means taking living beyond your means to a new extreme.

Juliet Schor, sociologist and bestselling author of *The Overspent American: Why We Want What We Don't Need* (New York: Basic Books, 1998), calls it "the new consumerism."

She cites the fact that during the stock market and economic boom of the mid- and late 1990s, the top 20 percent of income earners became "conspicuous consumers," meaning the ways in which they were spending their wealth were visible to us all. This was due in part to the rock star status given to overnight millionaires, who capitalized on the technology-driven stock market boom and the real estate boom, which quickly followed.

In her book, Schor says that it was only a matter of time before *human nature* took over: "As a group of extremely high earners emerged within occupation after occupation, they provided a visible, and very elevated point of comparison for those who weren't capturing a disproportionate share of the earnings of the group. . . . Daily exposure to an economically diverse set of people is one reason Americans began engaging in more upward comparison."

It's Human Nature to Compare

In 1954, social psychologist Leon Festinger came up with the "social comparison theory," which is at the heart of many studies in sociology today. It says that *all* human beings actually have a drive or need to compare their abilities and opinions. Festinger believed that we evaluate ourselves by making comparisons with similar others.

Pearls from Planners

"The first step is to get over yourself and have a good laugh, as EVERYONE but the rare saint is involved in social comparison. We're social animals. Fitting into the group and establishing rank are essential components of every human group. Not only are we all comparing ourselves—if only slyly—to the Joneses, but we are also trying to not be too different from them."

Vicki Robin, coauthor of *Your Money or Your Life* (New York: Penguin Books, 1992) asked me to pass along this note as we examine the "Jones" dynamic.

While our comparative natures explain some of the reason we put time, energy, and money into having everything the Gateses have, when you really talk to people about this phenomenon, it becomes clear that good old-fashioned *fear* is at the heart of much of our drive to keep up—fear that our kids won't have the *best* education possible, like the Gates children; fear that if we don't have the *best* material things like our neighbors, we're not as successful as they are. The list goes on and on.

There is nothing wrong with wanting what's *best* for you and your family. One of the many unfortunate side effects of fear, however, is that it is blinding.

Life Planners say a major reason we don't live out our goals and priorities is that we are unconsciously trying to live up to the Joneses' and the media's definition of "best."

We put time, energy, and money into living out those definitions, while turning a blind eye to our own values.

Pearls from Planners

"Most people are basically unconscious about that influence. It gets drummed into us so consistently, and from such an early age, that it's just a part of what we experience as 'normal' surroundings and our culture. We don't think about it, we just accept it. We behave or respond based on those messages without bringing a conscious part to that decision making."

Barbara Culver, Life Planner; author; founder, Resonate Inc., on "keeping up with the Joneses"

Your Best

Let's make sure that you're channeling your time, energy, and money toward your values, and not those of the Joneses or Gateses. We'll start by getting an idea of how much time, energy, and money your current lifestyle is costing you.

Please answer the following questions:

- How much money do you make each hour that you work? If you don't get paid by the hour:
  - ◆ Take your net income. Divide it by the number of days you work per year:
    Example: \$35,650/240 = \$148.54
    This person makes \$148.54 per day.
  - ◆ Take your daily income. Divide it by the number of hours you work per day. (Hours worked can vary, so just use your best approximation.)
    Example: \$148.54/8 = \$18.57
    \$18.57 is this person's hourly wage.

Use the chart on page 38 to organize your answers. You'll see a column titled "Reexamine." Leave it for now. We'll fill it in shortly.

- Based on the amount of money you make per hour, how many hours does it take to pay your monthly housing payment (mortgage, rent, etc.)?
- Divide the expense by your hourly wage.
  Example: $600/$18.57 = 32.3 hours
  A $600 mortgage would require about 32 hours a month of work if you were earning $18.57 an hour.
- Do the same for the following:
  ◆ How many hours of work each month does it take to pay your monthly car payment, if you have one? (If you pay to store your car at a garage, for example, include that as well.)
  ◆ Think about other big assets that you own. Let's call big assets those worth more than $1,000. This can range from the latest, hottest, flat-panel TV to a second home. List those assets, and determine how many hours of work it takes each month to pay for them.
  ◆ Think about your assets that require maintenance (house, car, boat, etc.). Try and determine how much you spend on maintenance on a monthly basis. (If something requires yearly maintenance, divide that number by 12 so that we can work it into this glimpse at your monthly time and money expenditures.)
  ◆ If you have children, how many hours of work does it take each month to pay the monthly costs for their education (if you pay more than what's covered by your taxes for public education—for example, private school tuition)?

Pearls from Planners

Life Planner Richard Vodra says one of the biggest challenges he runs into when it comes to "rescripting clients" regards educating their children. Many will send their kids to private schools and colleges that they simply can't afford, without examining what they want their child to truly get out of an education. One solution that is working for many of his clients: taking a portion of the money they would allocate to education and using it on tutoring, travel, and cultural events. Some clients are also encouraging their children to get involved in volunteer

(Continued)

work. Many see this type of education as being more aligned with their values, and it doesn't send them to the poor house! If they have a real concern that their child will not have the economic advantages society tells us are attained through an expensive education, Vodra suggests that parents take some of the money they would use on schools and invest it for their children. The financial benefits of a long-term investment will give children many economic advantages.

- How many hours of work does it take each month to pay monthly cost of clothing for you and/or your family unit?
- How many hours of work does it take each month to pay for the monthly costs of you hobbies for you or your family unit (e.g., tennis, music lessons, golf)?
- How many hours does it take to pay for your or your entire family's monthly social activities and entertainment (e.g., dining out, movies)?

Expense	Total Monthly Cost	Work Hours to Pay	Reexamine
Example: Mortgage	$600	32	
Mortgage			
Car			
Big assets			
a.			
b.			
c.			
d.			
Asset maintenance			
Education			
Clothing			
Hobbies			
Social activities			

The Nonmaterial

Now that we've examined the time spent on the material part of your lifestyle, let's look at the time you devote to nonmaterial things. There is a chart on page 39 to help you organize your answers. Again, we'll get to that "Reexamine" column in just a moment.

- How many hours do you spend at work each month? (Just multiply the number of hours you spend at work each day by the number of days you work each month. For many of us, that number is 20.)
  Example: 8 hours a day × 20 days per month = 160 hours spent at work each month
- How many waking hours do you spend with your family each month? Think about how much time you spend with your family each day, and on weekends, to come up with your best weekly estimate. Multiply that by 4.
  Example:
    3 hours with family each weekday = 15
    12 hours with family on weekends = 24
  This person is spending 39 hours with her family each week × 4 = 156 hours/month.
- How many hours do you spend socializing with friends each month?
- How much time do you spend on hobbies and activities you enjoy each month?
- How much time do you spend on self-improvement each month (e.g., going to the gym, massages, reading)?
- Think about the goals and priorities you identified in Chapter 3. How much time do you spend each month to bring you closer to those most important goals? For example, you might spend 1 hour each weekday, about 20 hours a month, taking public transportation in order to save money for your personal goal of going to Australia.

Event	Monthly Hours Spent	Reexamine
Examples:		
Work	160	
Family Time	156	
"Goal Tending"	20	
Work		
Family		
Social/Entertainment		
Hobbies		
Self-Improvement		
"Goal Tending"		

Are You Living Your Ideal Relationship with Money?

As you look at how you're spending your time and money, you want to think about whether your choices in these areas are in alignment with your values. Look over the previous two charts. If you see areas where there's a disconnect—expenditures that just don't seem worth the time it takes to pay for them or areas of your life that would benefit from more time—put an "X" in that reexamine column.

For example, would your children benefit from the extra time you could spend with them each week, if you didn't have to devote so much time to making money to pay for some of your expenses? I know many planners who have helped their clients make arrangements to do things like job share and telecommute, in order to achieve their parenting goals. They couldn't even see these as realistic options because they were so caught up in how they thought they had to live and fulfilling those obligations.

What could possibly be so important that it is prompting you to take time away from the areas where you really want to devote it? What belief is allowing that behavior to occur? Really think about this because examining and figuring out how to change it, or tame it, is what will bring about the changes you're looking for.

Planner Rick Kahler told me about a client who was overspending by 20 percent each month. She was spending money she didn't have to "keep up with the Joneses" and send her child to a private school. She truly believed that the only thing you can give your kids that can't be taken away is a private education. That was her rock-solid belief; therefore, her behavior made perfect sense.

He had the client reexamine that belief. Interestingly, she didn't even know that she was carrying it, let alone acting on it, until he pointed it out. Because of this new awareness, she was able to connect with her *real belief,* that there are other ways to ensure her children's lasting well-being, and other education alternatives that won't be such a drain on her financial resources. They examined what she wanted her children to get out of an education and came up with creative, less costly ways to help them achieve it.

Planners also say that social scripts take time and money away from our most important personal goals. Would a goal of starting a business, for example, have a better chance of becoming a reality if we were making the monthly payments on a $15,000 car versus a $30,000 car (like the Joneses), and reallocated that money toward that goal?

Think about how your life would be different if you weren't under pressure to "keep up." How would you spend your time? How would your relationships change? How would you feel about yourself? If you really don't believe the pressure to keep up is at work in your life, think about the beliefs that allow you to resist it. In either case, take some notes. We'll use them later.

_____

_____

_____

_____

_____

If you're interested in examining more ways to align your spending with your priorities, The Center for a New American Dream (newdream.org), is a great resource!

Gender Scripts

I once interviewed a woman who grew up in the Midwest in the 1960s and 1970s. Her mother made all of the big financial decisions in her family. Her mom did the accounting, the saving, the planning, and so on. Her father didn't even have a checkbook.

The reason this woman comes to mind as we start this discussion on the messages society sends us about gender is that she was one of a handful of women whom I've come across in my reporting, and my life experience, for that matter, who grew up in a family where a woman made the major financial choices.

Not only do the majority of the women I've met have a lack of role modeling in their family structures, but they're also battling tremendous social pressure to take a backseat when it comes to taking control of their personal finances.

On the flip side, men typically don't have a model for sharing financial responsibility, without somehow feeling like they're not living up to what's expected of them.

A society that pays a man about 25 percent more for doing the exact same job as it pays a woman is sending a pretty clear message about which of the sexes is expected to have bigger financial responsibility! (Labor Department data analyzed by the Economic Policy Institute says that in 2005, college-educated women between 36 and 45 years old earned 74.7 cents in hourly pay for every dollar than men in the same group earned.)

There is an actual saying in the financial community among some money managers, when a couple comes in for counseling— "Don't pitch the bitch." The thought is that women will ask too many questions and need too much hand holding, and consequently, the manager will have to work harder. Another consequence of this stereotyping is that the man has to work harder than the woman to understand the financial choices the planner is offering. They're coming to him, not his wife. The burden is on him.

While the "men are breadwinners" message may be softening— surveys show that working wives contribute more than a third of the typical family's income—planners say the "men handle the money" dynamic is alive and well in their client's financial behavior.

The Dangers for Men

The days when long-term financial planning meant putting a piece of your family's savings into IBM or General Motors stock are long over (not that those are bad investment decisions as part of an over-all plan). Financial planning has become a complicated business. There are many options and variables out there—many investment choices to make, many risks to consider.

The societal expectation that men who are not money managers by profession can make these big, complicated financial decisions by themselves is completely disconnected from the realities of managing money today.

Experts say the real problem and danger with this scripting is that the pressure on men to understand complex financial issues is so strong that it has fostered a reluctance to seek help and ask questions.

Pearls from Planners

"If men can understand that they have an unreasonable burden placed on them ... perhaps there was a time during their great grandparent's or parent's eras when finances were simpler, and they could be expected to know more. Now, the financial world is very complicated. They may want to reconsider the original message, and be open to other ideas. Don't be afraid to ask for help is the message we should be sending."

Peg Downey, co-founder Money Plans; selected as one of Worth magazine's top financial advisers

Men, How Are These Influences Affecting You? Men, please think about the following questions, and take some notes. Ladies, this is interesting "food for thought" for you as well.

- What are your thoughts on the belief by many experts that society expects men to be financial experts? Do you think that expectation is unrealistic given all of today's complexities when it comes to investing?
- Do you ever see this societal script, that you should have a great deal of financial expertise, at work in your own behavior? If so, how? If not, how have you been able to overcome it?
- What are some of the other big messages you feel society sends when it comes to men and money? For example, many feel pressure to be the breadwinners.
- Do you ever see the messages that you've observed at work in your own behavior? If so, how? If not, how have you been able to overcome them?
- Did a man or woman make the big financial decisions in your household when you were growing up? Do you see this playing out in your own behavior?
- What are the pros and cons?
- Do you make the big financial decisions for yourself or your household? If so, do you think you're qualified to determine if your financial choices are the best ones, when it comes to achieving your goals?
- If you are making the big financial decisions for a family, would they be prepared to take control of the finances if you were out of the picture? What do you think of this?
- If you're not responsible for a family, is there anyone who would know how you want your finances handled if you were out of the picture? What do you think of this?
- If you're acting on some societal messages about gender, do you think rewriting them would better serve your best interests?
- How would you rewrite them to reflect your true beliefs? How would this play out in your behavior?

Keep your notes handy. We'll use the information when we put together "Your Story" at the end of this section.

_____

_____

_____

_____

The Dangers for Women

In 2002, I appeared on *The Oprah Winfrey Show* to discuss the financial issues that face women. My segments were taped, so I didn't have live interaction with the women in the audience. As I went back and listened to what they were saying, however, I was struck by the insecurity and hesitation in their verbal and nonverbal language. These very capable mothers, working mothers, professional women, and the like were very unsure about their capacity to manage money.

Planners say women don't take the lead when it comes to making big financial decisions for two major reasons:

1. They lack confidence in their ability to manage money.
2. They lack knowledge about personal finance.

They say that lack of knowledge is a direct result of not giving themselves, and not being given, the experiences with money that would build their self-esteem.

Pearls from Planners

"A lot of my work with women is pointing out that they're very capable. They don't give themselves credit for the financial decisions they make, and use those as building blocks to make bigger decisions. I'm constantly hearing, particularly with women 45 years and older, "I don't know anything about money." That's wrong, and when I have them sit down and spend some time trying to understand things like investing, it's always a lot easier for them than they think."

Tiffany Bass Bukow, founder, MsMoney.com (a great resource for women and personal finance issues)

The funny thing is that women tend to be better investors than men! I did a story for the *CBS Evening News* in the late 1990s about how female investment clubs outperformed male investment clubs.

The National Association of Investment Clubs said the women's clubs outperformed their male counterparts by a wide margin in 9 out of 12 years! Analysts cited as the major reasons for their success the fact that women tend to take time to do research, they aren't afraid to ask for help, and they tend to hold investments for the long term.

Unfortunately, the women in these investment clubs are not the norm. Planners say many women think investing in financial markets involves too much risk. When you consider the following, however, you'll see that the *biggest risk* is in not taking control of your financial future.

- Forty-four percent of women 65 and over are widowed. Fourteen percent of men 65 and older are widowed. (*Source:* Population Resource Center)
- Almost one in four women are broke within two months of their husband's passing.
- Women live longer, so they need 20 percent more for retirement.
- Women take off approximately 11 years more from work than men (to raise children and care for parents). That means they have less income to apply toward retirement savings.
- Less time in the workforce means Social Security benefits are about half that of men's.
- Eighty-seven percent of poverty-stricken elderly are women.

(*Source:* MsMoney.com)

Women, How Are Societal Messages Affecting You?   Women, please think about the following questions, and take some notes. Men, just as the women reading this book may have gained some insights from your questions, you may find thinking about these issues enlightening.

- When you look at the previous statistics about some of the financial realities facing women, what are your thoughts on social scripting to let men handle big financial issues?
- Do you see any of the messages about women taking a backseat to men in financial dealings at work in your life? What do you think of this?
- Did a man or woman make the big financial decisions in your household when you were growing up? Do you see this playing

out in your own behavior? If so, who is making the big financial decisions for you—is it you, a spouse, relative, friend, professional, etc.?

- What are the pros and cons of having this person make your important financial choices?
- Do you know if you have enough saved for retirement and emergencies to achieve your goals in these areas? What do you think of this?
- Do you know how the money you have is working to help you achieve what you've identified to be your most important goals? For example, do you know how it's invested? What do you think of this?
- What areas of your financial life would you like to change? Would you like to save more, invest more, etc? Are you in control of these decisions?
- If you are not solely responsible for your finances, would you be prepared to take control if something happened to the person who is? What do you think of this?
- If you're not happy with your last answer, what can you do now to change that? How would your beliefs and behaviors be different?
- Think about some of the financial decisions you make. What skills do you exhibit? What are the things you do well?
- Think about your ideal relationship with money. Perhaps you would like to be more in control of your finances. Maybe they would be reallocated to help you achieve your most important goals. What would be different about your current behavior to make this vision a reality?
- Which of your scripts need to be rewritten in order for you to have the relationship with money that you desire?

Keep your notes handy. We'll use the information when we put together "Your Story" at the end of this section.

_____

_____

_____

_____

_____

Messages About Ethnicity and Race

I know a woman whose mother recently passed away. A few days later, her brother had a heart attack. Both her husband and daughter were diagnosed with cancer during that same month. She was balancing all of this grief and trauma with running a catering business and restaurant.

In addition to running to doctor's appointments with her husband and daughter and organizing her mother's estate without wanting to lean on her sick brother, she was opening a second restaurant. This woman also did not belief in hiring assistance for help with things like household duties.

I begged her to take some time off. Her family had large financial resources. She said there was no time for rest, and joked that it was her "Italian work ethic" that was driving her. "We're taught that there's pleasure in suffering!" she said.

We laughed, but I could tell that she not only thought there was truth in her words, but on some level, she was experiencing gratification by living up to what she thought was expected of her. Maybe the "workhorse" message served her when she was getting started in the restaurant business, but it clearly did not serve her well-being at this time.

I couldn't help but think how much easier her life would be if she weren't programmed to act on that deeply embedded belief.

A doctor I was speaking to a few years ago realized that social expectations were a large part of the reason he was "living the life of a responsible WASP," as he put it. The remark came up because I was telling him about a friend who made a great living at her passion, teaching yoga and massage. She lives and works in a beautiful villa in the Caribbean across the street from the ocean. Her rent is about $700 a month, and she has more in savings than many of the "9-to-5ers" I know. I'll never forget his response to her story: "Nobody ever told me that was an option."

There are groups who are perceived to be responsible when it comes to finances. There are groups who are perceived to be untrustworthy. There are groups who are perceived to be overly frugal. The lists go on and on. Planners say most of us are unaware of how big a role these scripts play out in our own behavior. We rarely give them much thought. Like the doctor I mentioned, these messages can program us to think that our options are limited, and that we are confined to certain behaviors and choices.

Pearls from Planners

"These expectations we put on ourselves and the outside messages we receive have a really strong influence on our behavior. I would urge people to look at those influences and ethnic messages. Ask: Is this how the world really is, or is this just how I see it? To create change, you have to be mindful of that, and follow your own common sense. Again, be mindful, and create change. Don't let stereotypes weigh on your self-esteem."

Martin Siesta, Life Planner, Compass Wealth Management

In addition, we are constantly fed messages by the media and marketing machines of the world that reinforce the stereotypes with the images, services, and products targeting one group versus another.

Self-Fulfilling Prophecies

Stereotyping is incredibly dangerous on all levels, financial issues being no exception. The person doing the stereotyping is confined to a narrow range of choices for engaging with an individual or circumstance. The person being stereotyped is often limited to a narrow range of options.

Buying into social scripts about groups and individuals can often lead those stereotypes to become self-fulfilling prophecies!

I've seen this firsthand in the numerous stories I've done about the financial challenges that minorities face.

There is a stereotype that blacks and Hispanics are bad financial risks. In fact, a study conducted by the Federal Reserve in 2006 found that Hispanics were denied home loans at a rate of 21.3 percent, versus a 12.2 percent rate for white applicants.

Massachusetts Congressman Barney Frank was so appalled by the study's findings that he remarked, "It is unacceptable for a nation committed to ending racial and ethnic disparity in financial services to allow this to continue." The Fed said in its analysis that lenders might not even be present in some neighborhoods that have large minority populations, or that they might not promote loans in those areas!

Similar studies have uncovered a huge propensity for lenders to offer minorities sharply higher interest rates for the same loan they would give to a white borrower. Many Wall Street analysts I've interviewed also say minorities are targeted for subprime loans and their sometimes explosive costs and interest rates.

"This breeds a lack of trust and frustration on the part of many minorities, often times leading them to avoid, the very financial institutions that could help them, educate them, and empower them with the confidence to challenge the system," Derek Douglas, associate director for economic policy at the Center for American Progress, told me during an interview.

"Until that trust is restored, the messages we hear about these groups and money will become self-fulfilling prophecies in many instances," he added.

Breaking the Cycle

Think about some of the stereotypes that are associated with your race and ethnic group. Write them down.

_____

_____

_____

_____

_____

- What do you think about these "social scripts"? What do they say about your group when it comes to financial behavior?
- What financial behaviors do you see people "like you" displaying? Think about things like debt, saving, investing, taking control of their financial choices, and giving to charity.
- What financial behaviors do you see people "like you" not displaying?
- Are the perceptions and behaviors of people in your group consistent with who you are, or could they be limiting in terms of the goals you want to achieve in your financial life?
- Do you see these perceptions at work in your own life? Is that a good thing for you in terms of reaching your goals or a bad thing?
- Are there any areas in which rewriting those scripts would best serve your interests? How would your behaviors change?

_____

_____

_____

_____

_____

Your Story

Living a Financial Life that Is Free from Social Pressures!

It's time to tell "Your Story" when it comes to societal scripts. As you've learned from the work you've done in this chapter, a lot of effort goes into preparing for a news story! You now have the information you need.

This is the story of *(your name)*, a person who is creating a life of which we all can be envious! *(Your name)* is breaking away from the pressure that many of us feel to "keep up with the Joneses," and the pressures to behave in a certain way due to *his/her* gender. *(Your name)* is also distancing *himself/herself* from social stereotypes about *his/her* race and ethnic group.

In order to detach *himself/herself* from social pressures to live in the right neighborhood, drive the right car, send *his/her* children to the right school, and the like, *(your name)* had to reexamine *his/her* own beliefs about:

_____

_____

_____

_____

_____

When *(your name)* imagines a life in which *he/she* is living in step with *his/her* values, *he/she* needs to make the following to changes to the ways in which *he/she* spends time and money:

_____

_____

_____

_____

(Your name) *has/has not* seen some of the social expectations about *his/her* gender at work in *his/her* financial choices. (If so), *he/she* thinks making the following adjustments to *his/her* behavior will make a better statement of who *he/she* really is!

_____

_____

_____

_____

_____

(_Your name_) is aware of some of the ways in which social messages about race and ethnicity can play into our behavior. _His/her_ group(s) are scripted to think _____

_____

_____

_____

about their abilities to make and manage money.

(_Your name_) believes that these messages _do/don't_ serve _his/her_ best interests. _He/she_ needs to take the following actions to _change/build on_ the behaviors that are a result of those "scripts."

_____

_____

_____

_____

We here at the station applaud (_your name_) on _his/her_ efforts to create a life that is free from social pressures and in line with _his/her_ priorities!

Moving Forward

Think about those areas where you resist societal pressures. Think about how this makes you feel. Strong? A sense of pride? Now think about some of the areas where you could benefit from distancing yourself from social influences. Reconnect with that feeling of strength you just conjured up.

Do your best to remind yourself of that feeling every time you run into a tendency to give in to a societal message. Simply remind yourself that you do have the strength not to give in; consequently, you can make different choices. Notice how this makes you feel. Notice if your experiences change.

We'll talk more about how to make some of the changes you desire in Chapter 9, but for now, try those simple reminders.

CHAPTER 6

The Songs We Play in Our Heads

I know a woman who is always complaining about the ways in which people try to take advantage of her when it comes to money. Whether it's a family member wanting to borrow it, her stock broker trying to convince her to invest in things just so that he can "get a fat commission," the government, or the grocery store checkout boy trying to give her the wrong amount of change, this woman is convinced that *everybody* is trying to "get one over on her."

This belief would come out in one form or another in virtually all of her financial dealings. She would always question people's motives, unconscious of the fact that she was also questioning their character. Consequently, she rarely got a warm reception, and some people probably used her bitterness as a justification to take advantage. This reinforced her negative thinking.

What struck me was that each time she talked about the latest ploy to get her money, it was as though someone pushed a play button on a tape recorder. Her words were always the same.

Her niece wants to borrow money. "What does she think, I'm an idiot?" Her broker has an investment idea—rewind the tape: "What does he think, I'm an idiot?" Her taxes go up—rewind the tape: "What do they think, I'm an idiot?" She didn't even realize how consistent her reactions were when financial issues came up.

This message brought so much misery into her life—it seemed like it was all she ever thought and talked about—that I couldn't help but think how her world would change if that little tape recorder in her head played a different tune, or if she could at least turn down the volume.

Imagine if this woman's song were "I'm an intelligent person, and no one can take advantage of me unless I let them." She might be able to approach situations with an openness that would allow her choices to be based more in reality than in fear and insecurity. She'd be less insulting to people, and her experiences would change.

The Song Remains the Same

We all have various "songs" that play over and over again in our heads, like that "What does he think, I'm an idiot?" tune. These tunes color our words, feelings, attitudes, and perceptions. I've been able to observe this closely when it comes to financial issues for two reasons: (1) journalists learn to pay close attention to the words people choose, and (2) money is a highly charged issue. People sing many songs about it.

When I talk to various experts about this, they say there is usually a big event, or events, in our life that lead us to create the thought and lay down the tracks for our various songs. These thoughts can also come from familial and social scripting.

It is human nature to try and protect ourselves, so, when a similar situation comes up, the brain goes into defensive mode and repeats the thought. Before long, a habit is formed. Psychologists say each time we act in that same way, the pattern is strengthened and reinforced.

The problem is that while the thought may have been appropriate in a few situations, we bring the same old song to every scenario that triggers the same emotion. Those messages not only affect our behavior, but ...

The same old song usually gets the same old results!

Planners and psychologist also point to the human tendency to have critical and negative thoughts. There is an inner critic in all of us, singing songs of judgment on almost everything we do: "You'll never be rich." "You never get the credit you deserve." "He's not really going to call." The tunes go on and on.

Pearls of Wisdom

"Confrontation seldom works to quiet the critical self because it is oriented toward having power over you. It enjoys the conflict. ... I learned early on in my writing that my critical self was destructive to my creative process if it yammered at me while I was writing. But it was valuable in the editing process. I got a visual image of what my critical self looked like and had mental conversations with her. I explained what I knew to be true and how I needed her to function. I also firmly stated that I would not tolerate any deviation from the behaviors I was prescribing for her. She tested my resolve until I had no choice but to put her into a burlap bag—I chose burlap because she could still breathe—and set her outside on the balcony. I told her I would invite her back inside when I needed her. And mentally I did just that."

C. Diane Ealy, *The Complete Idiot's Guide to Spirituality in the Workplace* (Indianapolis, In.: Alpha Books, 2002)

Our inner critic would have us believe that if we focus on what's wrong with a situation, the results will be more positive.

It is these critical songs, however, that are the very tools of resistance! The chorus is the same for all: "Don't change a thing. It won't make a difference anyway." The songs verbally give us permission to act on the limited visions we have of ourselves and our choices.

Pearls from Planners

"The habitual messages you tell yourself affect behavior. They usually contain words like *always, everybody, nobody,* and *never.* Also, statements of certainty, even if the word *certain* isn't there. 'My life would be great if it weren't for this one thing.' 'When this happens, everything will change.' 'When I have more time, everything will be different.' 'When I have more money, everything will change.' Once you have identified the habitual messages you tell yourself, ask: Is this really true? How do I know this is true? If it doesn't hold up to this reality check, it's time to change that thought pattern, or at least be aware of the discrepancy.

Oleg Gorelik, Life Planner; cofounder, Sheehan Gorelik LLC

"If the statement leaves no room for a dialectic and is one sided, it probably needs to be examined. Bring to it the awareness that it may have been true at one time - so you shouldn't be hard on yourself or judgmental—it just might not be a useful thought pattern right now. Just remember that your 'inner critic' is so explosive: give it any food, and it will run a mile!"

Andy Reed, Life Planner, Sheehan Gorelik LLC

"While you want to become aware of these powerful messages, don't get lost in trying to figure out where they came from, and whether they are true or not. Anytime something can be true in some situations and not in others, it's not where the truth is! It is productive and enlightening to go about the inquiry, but most important, realize this is something you are thinking about, not who you are."

Josephine Tempongko, Sheehan Gorelik LLC
These are excerpts from a group interview with the Life Planners of Sheehan Gorelik LLC.

Happy Songs

Habitual thought patterns can also be positive and productive. In my reporting, I've had the opportunity to interview countless successful people, ranging from heads of state to sports stars, celebrities, business icons, and stay-at-home moms.

One thing they all have in common is a positive, solutions-oriented way of thinking. They have practiced it so much that it has drowned out their negative tunes. The "This is going to hurt" song can no longer be heard over the "Here's how I can make the most of this" chorus.

Negative thoughts don't necessarily go away, but with practice, they can be almost instantly diffused by a positive, solutions-oriented way of thinking.

Pearls of Wisdom

"There is a practice called Cultivating the Opposite Emotion. To do this, we bring our attention to a positive emotion or feeling when negative sentiments come up. This is difficult and takes commitment, but commitment is something that is accessible to all of us. If you're in fear, put your attention on courage. If you can't forgive someone, cultivate what life would be like if you forgave that person. This doesn't mean you don't acknowledge your fears or that you condone that person's behavior. But by cultivating these positive images, like an actress does when she steps out of herself and into her role, we change our chemical reactions to those limiting emotions. We literally create a chemical and psychological environment inside ourselves in which new habits can, and will, be formed.

Ann Farbman Brown, therapist; founder, The World Yoga Center, New York

I had the honor of having a close friendship with someone who had to make the most radical transformation to his thoughts that I have ever seen a person have to make. It was a question of survival. The emotions and thoughts that Christopher Reeve had to deal with after his horseback riding accident are a testament to what the human mind and human spirit are truly capable of achieving.

Chris and I rode horses together for about 10 years. I was able to spend time with him on several occasions in the last year of his life. One day we were talking about one of the many physical ailments he was dealing with. He had just spent quite a bit of time bedridden and told me, "You never know how lucky you are to be in a wheelchair until you can't get out of bed."

Something welled up in me, and I screamed out, "How do you stand it! You do more good for people in this condition than healthy people do in a lifetime. How do you not just give up, or at least, feel sorry for yourself?"

He said, "Tell yourself you're pitiful and powerless over and over, and see how far that gets you. It makes you see that giving up is not a serious option if you're alive."

Chris just never allowed himself to indulge in negative thinking. He always told me that he, like many of us, tended to wake up in the morning with negative thoughts and fears. "I'll never get this done today." "I don't have enough time to do that." "I should have done this differently." "Poor me." He'd give himself an hour to let them run around in his head, and then that was it. He would not give them any more attention. It took a lot of time and practice to gain mastery over his thoughts. Still, as he always pointed out, if he could create new songs, so can you.

Top 10 Hits

Before we look at the messages you tell yourself and whether they are serving your best interests, take a look at what planners call "our favorite money tunes." They say these persistent, and often unconscious, thoughts lead many of us to act in ways that distance us from our goals. See if you notice any of them in your own thinking:

- I can't accomplish my dreams without more money.
- Money brings you happiness.
- One day, I'll have a big payoff (great excuse for debtors).

- Money is not important.
- When I have enough, I will help others.
- There will never be enough.
- Don't spend money.
- It's okay to go into debt. I deserve this.
- You have to work long and hard to get what you want.
- Rich people can't be trusted.

Dr. Ted Klontz, a psychologist who focuses on financial issues, shared with me his personal story to illustrate how the messages we tell ourselves about money can impact our behavior.

Dr. Klontz grew up on a farm in a very poor community in Ohio. He said his family never came out and literally sang the "Rich people can't be trusted" tune, but they always talked about wealthy people as if they took advantage of others.

In fact, he had a wealthy uncle who had the "audacity" to fly to family reunions and stay in hotels, instead of driving and staying with other family members like everyone else. His parents would talk about this uncle behind his back as if he were despicable.

At some level, Klontz wanted to make sure that no one ever talked about him like that. When financial situations would come up, the "Rich people can't be trusted" song would play in his head. He said society reinforces this message by often using terms for the wealthy, like *robber baron* and *filthy rich.*

As Klontz began to accumulate money in his own career, he would do things to sabotage his wealth.

"I would do something silly like buy 80 acres of land in the middle of Nowhere, Tennessee—things that would get me back into a 'financial struggle.' I knew that game. You struggle. You get creative. You make it work. I didn't know how to sit and feel comfortable with money," Klontz told me.

As he wondered how people feel okay about having more than what they need, he met a very wealthy woman, who sparked a shift in his thinking.

This woman told him she had a lot of money, and she felt good about it. No matter what happened, her children would never be financially obligated for her care. In addition, through her philanthropic efforts, she helped about 15,000 people a year. When she dies, her estate will be able to help another 15,000, and this will go on forever.

Klontz said this woman gave him a different way to view wealth. He began to realize he had been engaging in what he calls "poor thinking—I thought like a poor person."

This epiphany gave Dr. Klontz permission to change his tune about wealth. "You can be wealthy, and be a good person too" was his new song. He was able to turn down the volume when his inner critic started singing that same old song about rich people. That allowed him to drastically change his choices and improve his financial situation, without guilt.

It's All Inside!

The impact our internal messages have on our behavior is so strong that I couldn't help but wonder *why* we have thoughts and feelings that sabotage the very things that we want from life. Why are we constructed to bring skepticism and our inner critic into our thought processes, when they so often cloud reality and prompt us to work against our higher interests?

I think these thoughts and feelings are so strong because they are tools to protect us. Survival is, after all, our most basic instinct. It makes sense that we have tremendous psychological resources whose sole purpose is to keep us out of harm's way, even when that harm is more imagined than real. That makes it imperative to remember that our abilities to change, choose, and differentiate between what's real and imagined are even stronger.

We're not only constructed to survive, we're constructed to thrive!

It's a matter of directing our energy so that we use our abilities for our highest goals and ideas. We can use our discrimination, awareness, and ability to direct our attention to distance ourselves from those messages that are not in sync with who we really are.

Pearls from Planners

"We often begin to feel like something in us is broken, in order to think the things we do. I often remind my clients that they have the ability to become more aware, to make different choices, and therefore to change. One exercise that has helped my clients overcome negative emotions is to give their negative thoughts a physical form or a

(Continued)

name: naming them and really describing them as characters. What do they say and how do they say it? What do they wear? What do they eat for breakfast? Animating those thoughts and feelings allows them to disidentify with them, to be with them in a new, often lighter or humorous way, and gives them more freedom of choice in how to act, instead of using the same old knee-jerk response."

Tracy Toon Spencer, Life Coach; founder, Fertile Life Inc.

Your Songs

When we looked at the messages you received from your family and society, we simply had to look around. In order to look at the messages you tell yourself, we have to look inside. That's what the following series of exercises is all about. We will use them to help you identify the songs that play in your head when it comes to your finances and your goals. Then we'll put them through a reality check.

In order to identify those messages, you really have to tap into your ability to step back and *witness.* Just as we all have an inner critic, we also all have an inner witness. Thoughts and feelings are so seductive and powerful that it's easy to forget that we also have the ability to step out of them and watch events unfold. It's easy to forget that thoughts and feelings are things we experience, not the sum total of who we are.

A few years ago, I was taught the following exercise. I found it immensely helpful when it came to strengthening my ability to observe different thoughts, feelings, and behaviors without judging or criticizing myself.

Exercise

Sit in a chair with your feet flat on the floor and hip-width apart. Sit forward so that your lower back does not round and slump. You may want to put a small cushion between your back and the back of the chair. Fold your palms in your lap with the back of right hand resting in the left palm. You can also touch your thumb and forefinger, and rest them on your thighs. In either case, make sure your arms, from shoulder to elbow, hang straight.

Let your head relax and rise up in line with your spine. Relax your eyelids, cheeks, tongue, and the space between your eyebrows. Read through the following, then go back, close your eyes, and do the exercises. Don't worry if you have to open your eyes and refer to the book. Just make sure you go back, close your eyes, and give yourself time to let these realizations sink in.

- Notice the sounds around you, and the sensations that you are feeling. Notice the clothes against your skin. Notice the sensations that go with sitting—your thighs touching the chair, how your back muscles contract to hold up your spine. Are your cheeks and forehead tight? Do parts of you feel warm or cool? Now say to yourself, "I observe this body. If I can know my body, it must be outside me. I am aware of my body, but I am not my body."

- Next observe your breath. Notice how it flows in and out of your nostrils, and how it moves downward and expands in your lungs. Tell yourself, "I am observing my breath. Since I can observe the breath, it must be outside me. I am not my breath."

- Do the same with your energy. Are you tired? Fresh? Alert? Sluggish? Tell yourself, "I witness the state of my energy. It must be outside me. It must be other than me. I am not my energy."

- Now become aware of the flow of thoughts and images in your mind—the running commentary. Also, be aware of any emotions that arise and the underlying mood that prevails. Tell yourself, "I know my thoughts. I am aware of my feelings. I witness my moods. Therefore, they are external to me. I am not my thoughts and feelings, I am not my moods."

I also like noticing how particular thoughts trigger specific feelings and emotions. Our thoughts really do determine how we feel and what we experience. Learning how to manage your thoughts really changes how you experience life.

- Think of your feeling of "I-ness," your ego. Notice how there is a part of you that feels like a particular "me." "I am shy." "I am strong." "I am a good saver," etc. Say to yourself, "I am the knower of this feeling of I-ness. Since I am observing it, it must be outside me. I am not my ego."

- Meditators go on to ask: "Who is the witness of the body, the mind, the ego? Who is the knower?" and they wait to see what comes up. You can do this if you're so inclined.

- What we want to do for the purposes of this book, however, is to remember and strengthen your ability to witness without judgment. We want you to remember that there is more to you than your thoughts and the limited ways in which you identify yourself. As you sit for this exercise, remember your inner witness. Any time thoughts, feelings, physical sensations, or moods come up that serve as distractions, just acknowledge them, let the thought pass, and resume the exercise.

(Continued)

> I find it helpful to say tell myself: "I'm thinking" when I finally realize I've been swept away by a particular thought. It allows me to distance myself from it, and go back to witnessing.
>
> This exercise was taught to the authors by Sally Kempton, author of *The Heart of Meditation* (South Fallsburg, N.Y.: Siddha Yoga Publications, 2002).

If you really want to see what happens to all of those inner songs and thoughts when you step back and look at them, try this. Close your eyes and wait for your next thought. Bring your full attention to this. Just wait and see what thought comes up. That inner singer usually gets quite shy when you stop and take a look at what he's really all about!

Stay connected with your ability to witness as you think about the following questions. Take notes! We'll use the information when we put together "Your Story."

Think about your beliefs and the messages you tell yourself and others when it comes to your spending—not your *ideal* message or your *ideal* beliefs about spending. Think about the things you actually think and say about your *existing* behavior when a situation comes up that requires you to spend money: "I'll save more after this purchase." "This purchase will make me feel more important or accepted." "I deserve this, because of justifications x, y, and z."

_____

_____

_____

_____

_____

Let's do the same with other aspects of your financial life. What are your beliefs and the messages you tell yourself and others when it comes to your debt situation? Think about situations in which you accumulate and pay down debt. What are you saying to yourself?

_____

_____

_____

_____

_____

What are the beliefs and messages you tell yourself and others when it comes to saving? When you think about your savings, when you put money into it or take it out, what messages go off in your head?

_____

_____

_____

_____

What are the beliefs and messages you tell yourself and others when it comes to investing? What messages play when you think about your investment picture?

_____

_____

_____

_____

Highlight any positive messages you would like to build on. For example, "I would like to take the "Give it time" message of patience I bring to investing and apply it to the impatience my "I'll never be able to save" message brings me.

_____

_____

_____

_____

Do you have a partner, spouse, friend, or family member who would say you sound like a broken record when it comes to a financial situation? If so, what is the song they would say you always sing? I have a friend, for example, who says her husband starts every discussion about money with: "We're just not on the same page."

_____

_____

_____

_____

_____

What do you think of this song? How does it play out? In my friend's situation, the end result of her husband's song was that it would lead to disagreements. Not surprising, because he was bringing the same "We're not going to agree" dynamic to each of their conversations. That message was playing in his head while they were trying to have a discussion. It was so loud that he wouldn't even hear what she was saying.

Reality Check

Let's put your messages through a reality check. Think about the following questions.

First, let's revisit what Life Planner Oleg Gorelik shared earlier in this chapter. Do your messages contain words like _always, everybody, nobody,_ or _never_? Absolutes are a great hint that this is a mental rant and not reality.

- Do you notice statements of certainty like "My life would be better if I could just save more money" or "When I have more time, I'll invest more"?

  _____

  _____

  _____

  _____

  _____

- When you look at your thoughts and messages about your financial behavior, are they the truth? How do you know they are the truth? Are they based in reality or in things like fear, insecurity, and ego?

  _____

  _____

  _____

_____

_____

• What do you think of bringing the same old messages to new situations?

_____

_____

_____

_____

_____

• Do you see habitual thought and message patterns that you think bring you closer to your goals? What are they?

_____

_____

_____

_____

_____

• Do you see habitual thought and message patterns that may not be working in your best interests? What are they?

_____

_____

_____

_____

• Do you see ways in which the messages you tell yourself about money are playing out in your behavior? Think of Dr. Klontz. His "Rich people take advantage of poor people" message led him to act in ways that sabotaged his wealth.

_____

_____

_____

_____

_____

- Go back to Chapter 3 and look at your goals. Think about how your finances would look if you were to achieve those goals. Are any of the messages you tell yourself working against the actions you need to take in order to bring your finances and goals into alignment?

_____

_____

_____

_____

_____

- What messages would you be telling yourself and others if you were living your ideal relationship with money?

_____

_____

_____

_____

_____

Use your notes as we put together "Your Story" regarding the messages you tell yourself about money. We use these stories so that you have a concise point of reference when you literally account for what these messages are costing you in Part II of this book.

Your Story . . . In Tonight's Broadcast!

Borrowing a phrase from Dr. Norman Vincent Peale: "Change your thoughts, and you change everything!" Tonight a story of a person who is taking that message to heart!

(Your name) is taking the bold step of examining _his/her_ thoughts about money and financial behavior, so that _he/she_ can rewrite or distance _himself/herself_ from any messages that distance _him/her_ from the life _he/she_ really wants.

As _(Your name)_, examined the different aspects of _his/her_ financial life—spending, debt, saving, and investing—_he/she_ realized that the following thoughts always come up when certain situations arise:

_____

_____

_____

_____

_____

(Your name) realizes that the messages we tell ourselves can impact our behavior. After putting his/her habitual tunes through a reality check, _(your name)_ wants to sing a different song, so that _he/she_ will be free to make different choices when it comes to:

_____

_____

_____

_____

In order to do this, _(your name)_, will tell _himself/herself_:

_____

_____

_____

_____

when different financial situations come up, allowing for more clarity, when it comes to seeing all of _his/her_ options.

We here at the station applaud _(your name)_ on _his/her_ efforts! Examining the messages we tell ourselves about money is not only difficult, but it takes a lot of courage!

Moving Forward

Certified Anusara yoga teacher and wellness coach Jackie Prete asks clients to identify "the limiting thought" in various situations. What thought or message has to exist in order for you to move forward with a given behavior? Do you have to tell yourself "I'll never be able to save anyway" in order to move forward with a purchase that takes resources from your higher goals? Do you have to tell yourself "I'm not good at investing" in order to avoid this part of your financial life?

See if there are any limiting messages at work when you are in various financial situations. Ask yourself if they are true, or if they are based in our tendency to maintain the status quo. What would you tell yourself instead, if you were living your ideal relationship with money? Act on this message!

As Life Coach Tracy Toon Spencer suggested, try giving the old message a name or form. Tell yourself, "Here comes Mrs. Doubtfire again, in the bright red pants. What's that you're saying? You can't do this today? Well Mrs. Doubtfire, neither can you!"

Life Planning for Two

If you share your financial life with a spouse or partner and you haven't split up, run away, or locked them up and thrown away the key, congratulations! Think about the things we've discussed over the last few chapters, and just imagine all of the baggage we bring to the financial aspects of our relationships.

Couples of the opposite sex also have that whole Mars/Venus thing to contend with. Familial and social scripts may tell women to "clam up" when it comes to financial issues, going against a natural inclination to open up.

Men, on the other hand, are not only schooled to take the lead in financial issues, but they are also scripted to keep their emotions in check. There are tremendous emotions at play in our decisions about making and spending money. Life Planners say failing to address those emotional components leaves little chance of identifying the root cause of problem behavior, making it almost impossible for even the most fearless of leaders to change destructive patterns.

Communication—Fact or Myth?

All of the planners, therapists, and psychologists I've ever interviewed say that a lack of communication is at the heart of most conflicts about couples and money. That's perfectly reasonable because a lack of communication, which inevitably leads to a lack of understanding, is at the heart of almost every conflict between two people.

Still, it seemed to me that there was more to the story. I can think of many experiences in my own life when I've tried to open the lines of communication to resolve a disagreement. My best intentioned "We need to talk" has sent people running for the exits, or even worse, been taken as a call to arms. Many of the couples and individuals that I've interviewed about money report similar experiences.

There is clearly a lot that goes on in that gap between initiating a conversation and actually having it.

When I saw a book titled *How to Improve Your Marriage without Talking about It*, I couldn't resist an urge to explore its theories. If there were ways to improve a relationship that didn't involve talking, maybe it would give couples other options besides "the money talk." That talk was clearly not working for many of us, despite our best efforts.

The book was written by Dr. Pat Love and Dr. Stephen Stosny, who have more than 50 years of combined clinical experience. I was familiar with Dr. Love and asked her to share some of her insights. Her research has shown that these are the major factors that work against productive communication between men and women when it comes to money.

Pearls from Dr. Love

- Women talk to connect, men have to feel connected to talk. Many people start conversations about money when there is conflict. A sense of being connected was never present, and has little chance of being developed in a climate of animosity. Conversations about money tend to create more stress.
- Women hear concerns or complaints as an invitation to move closer. Men hear concerns or complaints as a warning flag that they are about to get blamed for something. That makes it very difficult to have conversations about money.
- Money brings us back to our primitive natures. Men are born believing they need to provide and protect. They manage their provider anxiety through control. That is a major reason so many control issues come up around money.
- Women participate in the provider side of the financial equation much more than they used to, but the belief that it is a man's job to take care of his family is still very prevalent in our society. That means women tend to look at how a man is providing to determine how much he loves her. That puts a lot of pressure on the financial aspect of a relationship.

None of this means that communication isn't the cornerstone of healthy financial relationships. What Dr. Love and many other experts that I've spoken to are saying is that there must be an understanding of what's causing communication problems in order to move beyond them.

The "I" in Integration

Understanding the differences in how men and women view financial issues is only half of the equation. As you've discovered in the previous chapters, factors like family scripting, messages from society, and our self-perceptions play a huge role in our financial behavior.

One planner told me the story of a couple who always fought about the amount of money the wife spent on clothes. The planner looked at the wife's early scripting. At that point the wife realized that a lack of clothing and money when she was growing up was working on her sense of self-worth as an adult. When she was young, this woman was picked on by other children and had vowed, on an unconscious level, that one day she would have the same nice clothes that the "special" people had.

The planner said this husband and wife both burst into tears and embraced when this belief came to light. Not only did the husband instantly develop a new compassion for and understanding of his wife's behavior, but she also developed a new compassion for and understanding of herself. Going forward, the husband had a new way of looking at his wife's inclination to buy clothes, and she had a new understanding of what prompted her to overspend.

You've put a lot of effort into understanding where your financial beliefs and behaviors came from. Now, it's important for your partner to do the same. Hopefully, he or she will be willing to go through the same process you are going through and do the exercises in this book.

In the meantime, the following questions will help them improve their understanding of where their beliefs about money come from:

- Who managed the money in your household? What role did the other partner play?
- Was there stress around money when you were growing up? How did you think that affected you?
- What would you say are your family's most important beliefs about money? Were their words consistent with their actions? How do you think this affected you?

- Do you think "keeping up with the Joneses" was important to your family? How do you think that affected you?
- What do you think about the fact that society still thinks it's the man's job to manage money? Do you think that plays out in our relationship? What do you think of that?
- What do you think are some of the stereotypes about financial behavior when it comes to your ethnic group or race? Do you see them at work in your behavior? What do you think of that?
- What do you think of your financial skills when it comes to saving, investing, and debt? What thoughts go off in your head when you think about these things?
- Do you think you use your financial skills in our relationship? What do you think of that? How do you think we could do things differently?

Don't forget to share your answers to these questions as well. As you discuss these issues, listen to each other. Ask questions; don't comment or criticize.

What Makes Them Tick

In addition to understanding your individual financial histories, you and your partner also need to understand each other's individual goals. You should respect and support each other's aspirations, even when you're creating goals as a couple or family.

Pearls from Planners

"People are much more receptive to valuing what the other person wants if their own wants are being valued. Once they've seen that they're both going to get what they want, they're relaxed, and then decisions can be made. This is common sense, when you're not caught up in emotion."

Patti Black, Life Planner, CFP, Charles D. Haines, LLC

If your partner is like most of us, he or she may need help when it comes to clarifying goals. Have them think about the questions from George Kinder that we looked at in Chapter 3.

- You have all of the money you will ever need, now or in the future. What will you do with it? From this moment forward, what will you do with your life? Your time?
- What would your life look like if you only had 5 to 10 years left?
- You've gone to the doctor and found out you'll be dead within 24 hours. The question is *not* what you would do with the time you have left, but what are your regrets? What do you wish you had accomplished in this precious life that is just about to end?

In addition to helping to clarify goals, these questions spark great conversations!

All of this brings us back, however, to the challenges of having "the money talk" in the first place.

Creating a Climate for Communication

Many of the planners and experts that I've interviewed say that the most important factor in creating a forum for communication lies in our actions, not our words. Most couples have spoken or unspoken agreements about money. They have an idea of what they are each expected to contribute to the unit. Even if it's not a financial contribution, they know what is expected when it comes to managing and spending. They have an idea of how they are expected to support each other financially or not, and they have an idea of the level of honesty that is expected when it comes to financial behavior.

Planners say the best way to open the lines of communication is to act in ways that honor these agreements. It's a question of respect and fidelity.

There may be things you want to change about your financial behavior as a unit, but don't expect your suggestions to be taken seriously if you have already proven that you don't keep your promises.

Having financial discussions during times of conflict is also a common mistake. We talked about this in our earlier discussion about Dr. Pat Love's research.

She tells women they must respect their male partner's belief that they must "provide and protect" when they talk to men about money. "Ask, 'When would be a good time to talk about our finances?' versus the standard, 'we need to talk,' she says.

"Also remember it's not just your financial life. Ask him to help you figure out a problem or a budget. Don't make it sound like you're the victim of an undesirable behavior."

Dr. Love reminds her male clients that for women, it's all about feeling close and connecting. "You can't hit her with, 'Why aren't you saving more money?' when you haven't paid her any attention in two or three days."

Women like to feel close. You can connect to them by talking and asking questions like:

- How can we best use our strengths?
- How can we make this a team effort?
- Tell me what you've been thinking about money.

In addition, affection goes a long way when it comes to connection!

Dr. Love adds that while men want to fix situations, when it comes to financial conversations, they must learn to stay quiet, and "Listen, listen, listen!" Not only will it help them to understand where their female partner is coming from; they'll also make their partner feel loved and valued.

Other advice from planners, experts, and couples who have created healthy relationships surrounding their finances include:

- *Have a monthly money meeting.* Life Planners say setting this time aside for your financial life is the key to having a healthy relationship when it comes to money. These meetings should be held in a quiet, intimate place, with a positive activity attached to it: a dinner out without the kids, a romantic dinner at home. If you think you are too busy to make time for this, planners say you are too busy! Think about the issues that your financial life represents: your dreams, your goals, your fears, your desires, your values, your beliefs, the things you want for your family. If you don't stay connected when it comes to these issues, you will be spending a lot more time fixing your relationship in the long run. Talk to your partner about this, and set a date.
- *Don't use money as a weapon.* A therapist once told me about a couple who came to her because they were having serious marital issues that stemmed from their finances. The wife felt that her husband was cheap, and he felt that she spent too much. She came from a wealthy family and was used to buying whatever she wanted. He came from a family that prided itself on being fiscally responsible. The husband was a bank manager, and their personal accounts were at his bank. The wife was constantly

bouncing checks. His colleagues were in the uncomfortable position of telling him each time she did this.

It wasn't that she didn't know how to manage money. The therapist helped them discover that she wanted to hit him where it hurt. She was mad that he yelled at her about her spending. She wanted not only to embarrass him, as he embarrassed her each time they had an argument about money; she also wanted to attack his core family beliefs about fiscal responsibility.

Planners say many couples use similar tactics in their own financial dealings. Both partners should look at the behaviors that are causing problems in the relationship, and identify where the anger is really coming from. To do this, they should look at the beliefs and scripts they use to justify that behavior, and give it a reality check: Is it true? Does it serve my priorities today? How do I really feel about behaving in that way? The key is to then determine how that script and the behavior needs to be adjusted to benefit the relationship.

- *Lose the notion that someone is right and someone is wrong.* There are no wrong beliefs and attitudes when it comes to money; there are simply *different* beliefs and attitudes. Think about your own scripting. Your beliefs come from your experiences. Your partner's beliefs come from his or hers. If you say you're right and they're wrong, you're essentially saying that your experiences, and your resulting beliefs, are more valuable. That's simply not the truth.
- *Get on the same page.* Each person should identify the "Top 5" values they think a couple should have when it comes to dealing with money. Look at areas where you agree, so that you can build on those. Discuss the areas where you don't agree. Look at where those disagreements are coming from. Is it different scripting? Where are the differences? Each partner should come up with at least three scenarios for compromise. Share them, and find the solution(s) that you can both live with.
- *Set short- and long-term goals.* Paint a picture of how you would like your life to look in six months. What are the things you would like to be doing? What are the things that you would like to be different? What about 1 year, 5 years, and 15 years down the road? What will your finances have to look like to reach those goals? What changes can you make in your individual behavior

to make the goals a reality? When one partner shares these changes, the other partner must just listen—without comment or criticism. Then, both can discuss what can be done as a couple to achieve these goals.

- *Tell each other what you value in the other's perspective each time you talk about money.* If one of you is a saver and one is a spender, instead of defending your position, tell the other person things you admire about that opposing quality. You might also like the way they execute some of the financial values that you share.

- *Make sure you each have your own money.* No two people have the same priorities around money. So when you're part of a couple or family unit, it makes sense to give each person an allowance. It should cover things like lunches, gas, cosmetics, haircuts, clothes, and other everyday incidental expenses. Your allowance is yours to spend however you want. Once you have agreed on amounts, that money is OFF LIMITS. If anyone wants to take the money out into the backyard and burn it, that's okay. Once decided, no discussion. A deal's a deal.

- *Identify positive and destructive patterns.* Each time many of the couples I've interviewed talk about their children, or their long-term goals, the gloves come off. Starting conversations about money with a glimpse into your future, or your child's future, could be very useful when it comes to creating a positive environment for conversation. As for destructive patterns, planners say many fights about money tend to happen at the end of the month, when people are preparing to pay bills. If you see this common pattern at work, you know what to do. Step away from the room!

- When conflicts come up, use the following four questions to guide your discussion:

  1. What's the problem?
  2. Where's it coming from?
  3. Why is it coming up now?
  4. What are the options to change it?

- *Don't talk about the financial behavior and attitudes of other family members unless they are really dangerous,* Comments like "You're just like your mother" will likely lead to discussions that have little to do with the financial issue at hand.

- *Be the ball.* This is for couples who have children and those who want them someday. Use the financial attitudes and behaviors you would like your child to develop to guide your own attitudes and behaviors. We'll talk more about this in the next chapter.

- *Remember that money is an aspect of your total relationship.* The same integrity and respect that you bring to issues in your marriage like sex, fidelity, and child rearing should also be present in your financial dealings. Like those other factors, ignoring integrity and your value system in your finances will have a domino effect on other parts of your relationship.

Think about what we've just discussed, and write down some of the ways you can create a better climate for communication with your partner. Ask him or her to do the same. You can use these notes to start the discussion at your first monthly meeting!

Many of the financial choices you make with Paula will be motivated by goals that you have with your partner. Let's put together the story of your relationship as a couple, so that you have a concise point of reference when you move into Part II. Make sure you get your partner's input. This is a story about both of you.

Your Story

Our Story ... In Tonight's Broadcast!

A story about love and money! (<u>*Your name*</u>) and (<u>*your partner's name*</u>) realized that if they were going to have a healthy relationship, they were going to have to have a healthy relationship when it came to money.

They started by reconnecting with their most important values as a couple when it comes to dealing with their finances:

In order to honor these values, *(your name)* is going to make the following adjustments in *his/her* own behavior:

_____

_____

_____

_____

_____

His/her partner plans to make some adjustments as well.

_____

_____

_____

_____

_____

This will be challenging for *(your name)* because of some of *his/her* deeply embedded belief(s). Those scripts are working against a healthy financial relationship with *his/her* partner. Those that are having the biggest impact on the relationship:

_____

_____

_____

_____

_____

(Your partner) also has some deeply embedded beliefs that don't serve the relationship:

_____

_____

_____

_____

_____

Still, their short- and long-term goals as a couple will provide them with the motivation to change. Their most important goals are:

_____

_____

_____

_____

_____

(Your name) needs to adjust the following behavior(s) to make those goals a reality:

_____

_____

_____

_____

_____

(Your partner's name) will make the following adjustments to *his/her* individual behavior to ensure that they achieve their goals:

_____

_____

_____

_____

_____

Together, this couple will do the following so that they can live the life they really want. (*Example:* Cut up one of the family credit cards.)

_____

_____

_____

_____

_____

In addition, *(your name)*, and *(your partner's name)* have set aside time to talk about their finances each month, so that they can stay connected to their goals and priorities.

There are ground rules when it comes to having productive conversations about money. This couple plans to take the following steps (look at that list of tips from planners in the previous section):

_____

_____

_____

_____

_____

We here at the station applaud _(your name)_ and _(your partner's name)_ in their efforts to take the necessary steps to make their goals a reality.

Moving Forward

Set up your first meeting with your partner. Together, come up with an environment that will make it very special. In addition, have your partner look at this chapter and do the exercises so that you both have an understanding of what you want to accomplish and how you plan to do it.

Creating a healthy financial relationship is very challenging, and you both may decide that you would like to enlist a third party's help. We'll discuss this option in Part III.

CHAPTER 8

Teach Your Children Well

Three themes have come up consistently in my research and reporting about teaching children about money:

1. Example
2. Experience
3. Communication

Planners across the board say children's deepest impressions about money will come from what their parents and caregivers do, much more so than what they hear them say. The old "Do as I say, not as I do" theory does not cut it when it comes to teaching children lessons about money.

That makes it imperative to set an example by conducting your own finances in ways that are consistent with the values you want to impress upon your child.

It is up to parents and caregivers to create real-life experiences for their children. They must create opportunities for them to learn about spending, saving, investing, philanthropy, etc. At this point in time, the majority are not learning these things in school.

Communication entails a lot more than just making broad generalizations about financial behavior.

A real understanding of the family's values, goals, and actions surrounding money must be present if the child is to adopt the beliefs and behaviors the parents and the caregivers feel are most important.

If you value living within your means, for example, make sure your child understands *why* you think it is important, as well as the *consequence of not doing it.* This will go a lot further than simply telling them: "Don't spend more than you make."

Adults also need to be clear and united on the financial lessons that they think are important to communicate. Planners say, even if they're not in 100 percent agreement, adults need to come up with five most important things they want to teach their children about money, and put up a united front.

The following questions will help you and your partner get on the same page when it comes to the important lessons you want to teach your children about money. They will also help those of you raising children alone to clarify your beliefs and values.

- What do we think is important for our child to know about saving money?
- What do we think is important for our child to know about investing?
- What do we think is important for our child to know about debt?
- What do we think is important for our child to know about charitable giving?
- How can we nurture the growth and development of these beliefs? What adjustments do we have to make in our own words and behaviors?
- What do we want our child to know about communication when it comes to financial issues? Are we demonstrating this in our behavior? What adjustments need to be made?
- Do we have money scripts that need to be rewritten? Are they playing out in our conversations and behaviors with our children? How can we do better in our words and actions?
- What are the financial situations we want are children to avoid? What's the best way we can express the dangers of these situations, while letting them know that we trust them to make sound financial choices?
- What are the things and activities that make our children happy? What role will money play in that equation—on our part and on theirs?

When to Begin

When should you start teaching a child about money? Planners say it varies, depending on the child's developmental level of readiness. Still, the earlier the better! Teaching your children while they're young will create a culture of conversation and openness in your family that will not only last throughout their teenage years, but will also impact the choices they make as adults.

Most say you can begin to lay the foundation for your children's future financial behavior when they are about four years old.

Acclaimed financial planners Joan DiFuria and Dr. Stephen Goldbart, cofounders of the Money, Meaning & Choices Institute, were generous enough to create the following guide for you:

Pearls from Planners

Age 4–8

- Start a "penny jar." Make it a big glass or plastic bottle. Your child will get a thrill out of saving until he sees that the container is full.
- Have your child count coins. Teach him what different coins are worth, and that small combinations combine to purchase things. For example, let's put together $1.50 and buy some crayons.
- Give your child exercises that involve making change.
- Introduce the concept of "need versus want." We need to buy food. You want to buy a toy.
- At approximately age seven, give your child a weekly allowance and have the child put the money into three containers: saving, sharing, spending.
- As a family, do a charitable activity: Take children with you to drop off clothes, food, or gifts.

Age 9–12

- Make your children aware of the cost of things—teach them the value of the dollar.
- Go to the grocery store with a certain amount of money, and tell your child that she needs to help you buy what is on the list. She can keep a running tab to see if you will have enough money to buy it all.

(Continued)

- Create or find small jobs that allow your child to earn money.
- Talk about saving and the idea of saving "for a rainy day."
- Have your child open a savings account, stop by to make deposits and withdrawals, get a tour of the bank.
- Chart the money the child earns.
- Pick two areas that are important to your child and make her aware of the costs: a desired toy, clothing, books, music, etc.
- Increase family charitable activities (food kitchen, church/synagogue activity).
- Have children pick 5 to 10 toys in good condition that they can give away to children who don't have gifts for the holidays.
- Have children regularly go through their closet and choose clothes they have outgrown, or don't use, and give them to children in need.

Age 13–15

- Comparison shop.
- Teach your teen about time and money (if Mom makes $10 per hour, how many hours of work did it take to buy groceries, lunch, taxi, etc.?).
- Put family bills on the kitchen table and review them with your teen.
- Teach teens about earning money for saving and spending: Expect your teen to work.
- Have your teen create budget and saving goals—college, car, insurance, etc.
- Have your teen read and understand bank statements.
- Introduce new financial concepts such as the need to pay taxes, why people have mortgages, and credit card interest payments.
- Let your children live with consequences of their financial choices, especially spending. (We'll talk more about this later.)
- Create a budget for discretionary spending (entertainment, cell phones, etc.).

Age 16–18

- Set an annual budget, with quarterly review, that your teen is required to manage.
- Give your teen the opportunity for trial-and-error learning.
- Review and expand savings goals: Have serious discussions about saving for a large, important purchase like a first car or sharing in the costs of their college education.

- Have them identify three causes they want to give to, and incorporate this into their budget. You can support them by offering things like matching contributions. We'll talk more about this in the next section.
- Expect teens to have some regular employment each year; at minimum, make sure they work for part of the summer.
- Teach them how to responsibly use credit cards. They can watch you if you don't want to get them their own.
- Teach the value of living within one's means.
- Teach the meaning of stocks, bonds, and mutual funds.
- Teach teens how earnings are affected by taxes and retirement savings.
- If your teen is interested, offer a limited amount of money to invest in the stock market, with the requirement that she learns to pick stocks and gets advice from a financial professional. Parents can fund the account and share the profits with their teen.
- Teach money values and social responsibility.

Joan DiFuria and Dr. Stephen Goldbart, Money, Meaning & Choices Institute

Stay Connected

Planners across the board say that the best ways to stay connected with your children's financial development and to guide them as they create a healthy relationship with money is the good old-fashioned family meeting.

Pearls from Planners

"Family meetings provide a forum where parents can share their views on what guides their financial decisions. Parents can hear how the children's values around money are developing. In addition, family meetings allow financial issues to get addressed before they become problems. Challenges can be tackled with thought, before things hit crisis level and become emotional.

Starting these meetings when children are young develops open communication around financial issues. It will help to foster an

(Continued)

openness and nonsecretive dynamic in many aspects of family life. In order to encourage this, parents should avoid telling children "This is how it's going to be." This can be perceived as a forced march. Families fare better when there's give and take, when everyone feels like they are valued—when everyone feels like they have a voice.

I often advise people to set up some meetings where no decisions are allowed to be made—they should just talk and think about their financial issues as a family—without the pressure and anxiety to come up with solutions."

Charles W. Collier, senior philanthropic adviser, Harvard University; author of *Wealth in Families* (Cambridge, Mass.: Harvard University Press, 2003).

Charles Collier and other family advisers say that it is important that family money meetings have a structure. Here are some suggestions:

- *Set a regular date.* When children are living at home, planners suggest you have weekly or biweekly meetings. Pick a time when everyone won't be rushed, and make it a fun event (a pizza party, popcorn time, etc.). Planners say if you don't stick to scheduled times, you are sending the message that financial issues are not that important. Also, pick a regular location. The thought of getting your teenager to actually sit down for a meeting may sound daunting, but planners say you'll be surprised. Money conversations are very important to teens, especially when they involve the amount they'll be receiving!

  When it comes to older children, planners say it's important to have quarterly or annual meetings. If location makes it necessary for some members to be there via telephone or computer, so be it. It is important that everyone understands the individual and family goals. If it's a group's desire to make sure that all the children in a family get a college education, for example, it's important that the grandparents understand what each of the parents want—they may want their child to pay for a portion of their schooling. It's also important that the parents know what the grandparents plan to contribute, so that they can be efficient in their planning.

  The same holds true with legacy and estate planning, as well as planning for elder care. Many families decide that a third party is necessary to help the unit make the most effective financial decisions. We'll talk more about that in Part III.

- *Pick someone to lead and set the agenda for the meeting. Rotate this person for each meeting.* This allows everyone to have a voice. It also allows quiet or more reserved family members and children to get comfortable talking about financial issues. Planners say to put even the smallest family members into this process. They may need help with the reading and writing, but it's important for them to feel involved.
- *Take notes.* Getting things down in writing somehow makes us feel that they are more real. Put your goals and plans of action down on paper. Notes can also help resolve future conflicts or debates.
- *Have everyone identify their concerns about money—for themselves and for the family unit.* In addition, get everyone's thoughts on what would alleviate these concerns and make them feel better. Questions like "Are we rich?" and "How come the Joneses just got a new BMW?" are likely to come up. This is a great chance to explain to your kids why you've chosen to spend your time and money on different things than the Jones family may have chosen. It's also a great chance to teach your children about your financial values. Remember, planners say kids need an understanding of why certain beliefs and behaviors are important if they are to truly adopt them.
- *Get everyone's thoughts on the family's financial behaviors that they like, and things they would like to see them do differently.* Jointly decide how those behaviors can be changed.
- *Be clear on your financial expectations of your children.* They need to know if you expect them to pay for a part of their education, for example, and they need to know how much you expect them to contribute. This can be a great opportunity to teach them about long-term saving and investing. Many mutual fund companies allow kids to contribute to their own education IRA (individual retirement account). In addition, there are funds set up specifically for children, which allow them to invest in small, regular increments. At companies like oneshare.com, your child can buy one share of stock. This can start him on the road to investing and watching the stock market. Planners say you should have your child set up specific savings targets. Tell him he can invest in Mom & Dad Inc., and his savings will be matched when

he meets his goals. It's a great way to start to teach children about investing.

- *Tell the family where things really stand with the family finances.* "This year, we're going to have to tighten our belts because we just bought a new house." "We can contribute $5,000 a year to your college education." It's up to you to decide how much detail you want to go into about your financial information, but above all, be honest!

I once interviewed a woman who was so concerned that her daughter understood the costs involved in going to college that she and her husband exaggerated how much of a struggle it would be for them to pay for her education. They were always talking about things like the need for her to do well enough in school to get scholarships and their expectation that she would pay for some of her tuition. They were never specific about what they could do.

This girl got accepted at her dream school, the University of Virginia, but she did not tell her family. She didn't want them to feel badly, and she was certain that the family could not afford it. This child convinced her family that she was thrilled that she was accepted at a cheaper girl's school, which had less of an academic curriculum. Her parents found out about this years later, and they were devastated! They could have definitely found a way to pay for UVA. Instead of being honest about how much they could contribute and creating a plan with their daughter, they tried to teach through fear. This is a mistake planners say many parents make.

- *Set goals as a family.* "We can go out to dinner three times this month." "If we all save specific amounts, we can go skiing next winter." Get suggestions on what family members would like to do as a family. Pick the two or three most popular ideas, and take a vote. It is important that children feel that they are part of the planning process. It's important for them to know that they have a voice when it comes to money.
- *Have everyone identify their individual financial goals.* A 16-year-old might want to save money to buy a car, for example. Identifying the goals will allow individual family members to know where everyone is coming from when it comes to making financial decisions. While all members can weigh in with suggestions on

how to help an individual achieve their goals, no judgment or criticism is allowed.

- *Meetings are a great opportunity to get your children thinking about the connections between money and happiness.* You can help them identify their passions and help them to begin to develop a plan to pursue them. Ask them questions like: What are your favorite subjects in school? What do you like about them? What are the things you like to do outside of school? What do you like about them? Are their ways we can build on the things you like to do? You love art class, for example; would you like to take a class at the museum about art? How much will that cost? How can we plan for that?

Pearls from Planners

Many of the Life Planners and psychologists that I've spoken to say asking children about the things that make them happy and exploring what they like about those things can offer them and you better clues as to where their passions are. They say this is more effective than the standard "What do you want to be when you grow up?" You don't want to open the door for things like "keeping up with the Joneses." You want to help them find work that brings them real joy and meaning.

- *Discuss the importance of charity and giving back at each meeting.* Identifying the charities to which the family would like to make contributions, and discussing why those charities are important to the group and to the individuals, provides an excellent opportunity to learn about your child's values and to share your own. Nonfinancial giving is an equally effective topic. Thinking of ways to volunteer and donate time is a great way to teach your child that there are more ways to be generous than just giving money.

As you can see, regular financial meetings are about much more than organizing the family's money. They are a chance to build bonds and an understanding of each other that will last a lifetime.

Kids Will Be Kids!

Okay, you've had the family meeting, and everyone feels warm and fuzzy, so why is your teenager screaming: "You don't love me! I need these!" when you refuse to buy him a $200 pair of sneakers?

Planners say the trick in these situations is to be as nonreactive as possible to this childish behavior. In addition, set limits and stick to them. Remember that you are the adult! Let your child know at a family meeting what you are willing to spend on their clothing and entertainment. If the sneaker allowance is $50 twice a year, he'll have to come up with any extra money that is needed, while still paying attention to his other spending and saving responsibilities.

Remind him, for example, that he still has to come up with $10 a month to help pay for college. Planners say these are the types of lessons that will teach kids the difference between want and need, and build responsible behavior when it comes to managing money.

What's Mine Is Mine—Yours Is What I Choose to Give You!

Kids will be kids, and some of them will conclude that it is dreadfully unfair for you to deny them an extra $50 for shoes when you just bought yourself a new top-of-the-line flat-screen TV. Remind them that you deserve that television. You've worked hard for it, and you put aside the money to get it.

Planners and experts across the board say one of the key elements in raising children who make responsible financial decisions is to teach them from an early age that you worked to create your lifestyle, and it's up to them to do the same. You want to avoid fostering a sense of entitlement in their financial beliefs and behaviors.

I report for a magazine for professional women called *Shattered: Breaking the Glass Ceiling*. I once did a story on a group composed of the most successful female entrepreneurs in the world. I interviewed Cheryl Womack for the story. She heads the organization Leading Women Entrepreneurs of the World, and made her first mark as an entrepreneur by creating an incredibly successful company that sells insurance to truckers.

Our conversation moved to family, and she told me her daughter once asked, "Are we rich?" Her response was: "No, *we're* not rich. *I'm* rich!"

Experts with whom I've shared that story say that was the right answer. In addition to helping children take responsibility for creating the lifestyle that they want, it opens up opportunities to talk to them about *why* they want that lifestyle. This is a great chance to help them align their values with their financial choices.

Your Family Story

Many of the financial choices you make with Paula will be motivated by goals that involve your family. Let's put together "Your Family Story," so that you have a concise point of reference when you move into Part II. Get your family's input. This is a story about all of you. It's a fun exercise to do as a group!

In today's report, making financial decisions as a family! The (*your family name*) family shows us how to do it, while staying connected to the family's most important goals and values.

In order to do this *parent(s), caregiver(s) name* had to identify what they felt were the most important things they wanted to teach their *child/children* about managing money. They were:

_____

_____

_____

_____

_____

(*Parents or caregivers names*) had to make the following changes to their own behavior so that they would be teaching by example:

_____

_____

_____

_____

That meant rethinking some of the beliefs and scripts that were driving their actions. They are:

_____

_____

_____

_____

_____

The _(your family name)_ family understands the importance of communication when it comes to sound financial behavior. In order to do this they are going to meet _(e.g., every Sunday evening at 6:00)_ to talk about the finances and the goals of the group, and the finances and goals of the individual members.

Some of the key topics the _(your family name)_ thinks are important to cover at these meetings are (refer to the suggestions in the "Stay Connected" section of this chapter):

_____

_____

_____

_____

In addition, the _(your family name)_ family will help the children in the family nurture their individual goals and passions by asking them questions that will help identify what makes them happy, and by helping them to create a financial plan so that they can help pay for the things they want to do.

Despite a parent or caregiver's best efforts, sometimes kids will just be kids. The adults in the _(your family name)_ family will take the following steps when their _child/children_ behave in ways that are financially irresponsible, or act out on a belief that they are entitled to certain things:

_____

_____

_____

_____

We here at the station applaud the _(your family name)_ for all of the work and effort to make sure that the ways in which their family behaves with money makes the grandest statement of who they are and what they stand for!

Moving Forward

As we've discussed, planners and experts say creating understanding and clarity when it comes to your financial beliefs and choices is the key to building responsible financial beliefs and choices in your children. This means they need to be clear on why you want to open up broader lines of communication by having things like family meetings. They need to be clear on why you feel these things are important.

And when it comes to those meetings, be sure to set up contingency dates for scheduling conflicts!

CHAPTER 9

The Truth about Change

Soon after my mother passed, my father and I had to have a meeting with her estate lawyer. Her estate was in good shape, but this lawyer also saw our gathering as an opportunity to show us how to organize our personal assets. He thought it was a good time for us to make sure that our wishes would be honored when our respective times came.

Everything he said made perfect sense. When I left that meeting, I had every intention of making sure that all of my 401(k)s were assigned to the beneficiary of my choice. I planned to create a will, name an executor, and so on. For some reason, however, I did not act.

I saw this estate lawyer a few months later, and he asked me if I had moved on his recommendations. He was very disappointed when he discovered that I had not. I can still see him shaking his head in disapproval.

I've met many people who have similar experiences in various parts of their financial planning. They walk out of a meeting with an adviser, with a new budget or investment plan, yet they do not put them into action. They are left with a deep sense of disappointment in themselves.

As we discussed in Chapter 2, we are given only two choices when it comes to claiming that we've been successful at making changes: action and inaction. When we fail to act, we're met with disapproval, and the "I'm a failure" song often starts blaring in our heads.

When I think of instances in my own life and the lives of others, where the intent to make a change was there but the action did not follow—it becomes clear that there are strong forces at play. There is a space between deciding to do something and actually doing it. Change, therefore, must be a process, and not simply "all or nothing."

I believe that if you really want to help someone make a personal change, you must help them in that space between action and inaction—that space where so many of us get lost. This is where I believe many of the personal finance techniques I've reported on let people down. Helping someone make lasting change means helping them through the change process itself—from beginning to end.

That's what this chapter is all about. It's my attempt to be there for you as you move through the process of actually changing your behavior, so that you can make your goals a reality. I felt that if I didn't help you move through that space between inaction and action, I'd be leaving you hanging, even if you did leave this book with your perfect financial plan.

With that in mind, I'd like to introduce you to the work of Dr. James Prochaska, Dr. John Norcross, and Dr. Carlo DiClemente. Dr. Prochaska is a professor of psychology and director of the Cancer Prevention Research Center at the University of Rhode Island. Dr. Norcross is a professor at the University of Scranton. Dr. DiClemente is a professor and chair at the University of Maryland, Baltimore County.

I was drawn to their work because instead of coming up with some magic "Five Easy Steps to Change," they looked from the outside in.

Prochaska, Norcross, and DiClemente spent years studying thousands of people who had been able to successfully change their behavior. They identified what those people had in common and what they did to make their changes last. After years of research, the professors discovered that:

Successful self-changers follow a predictable process, and use specific techniques to change their behavior.

Their research, which is chronicled in their self-help book *Changing for Good* (New York: William Morrow, 1994), is great news for all of us, and it has created nothing short of a revolution in the science of change.

Change is a complicated thing, so I ask you to bear with me. I've done my best to make their research and techniques as simple and understandable as possible in the pages that follow.

Dr. Prochaska, who initiated this study, became interested in finding ways to help people change their behavior after he watched his father lose his battle with alcoholism and depression. His selfless reaction to the loss of his father has helped countless numbers of people make the changes they desire. The types of changes we are discussing do not involve the painful physical and emotional withdrawals of substance abuse, but we can apply the same techniques to breaking destructive financial habits.

At some point, all change comes down to shifting habitual patterns.

Dr. Prochaska has been generous enough to share his findings with you.

The Changes that Will Help You Reach Your Financial Goals

Before we go any further, take a minute and think about the financial behaviors you would like to change within yourself. When you move into the next section with Paula, you will be able to get more specific. You'll see how your numbers are playing out, and you'll have a clearer picture of exactly what you need to do. For now, however, think about some of the things that you've learned about your financial beliefs and behaviors. Imagine how your life would look if you were achieving your goals. How would your actions be different?

In the following chart, I've listed different areas of your finances in the Financial Behavior column. In the next column, I'd like you to write down the Enabling Belief allowing you to maintain the status quo. In the scripting column, write "FS" if you see any family scripts at work in this belief. "SS" if you see any societal scripts at work, and "IS" for internal scripts, if any of the messages that play in your head are influencing your behavior.

In the final column, write the action you would be taking if you were living out your ideal relationship with money.

Financial Behavior	Enabling Belief	Scripting	Action
Example: Debt	Expect to be rescued	FS, SS	Create a realistic spending plan
Debt			
Saving			
Investing			
Retirement planning			
Legacy planning			

Keep these things in mind as we discover what it will take for you to make the changes you desire.

"Changing for Good"

Drs. Prochaska, Norcross, and DiClemente studied thousands of what they call "self-changers" in their efforts to identify what allowed them to successfully change their behavior. Self-changers are people who have changed without psychotherapy. Many of them have successfully reversed serious addictions to alcohol, drugs, cigarettes, food, and emotional distress on their own.

The doctors by no means have anything against therapy. Many people need assistance and guidance in order to change. **It can be argued, however, that therapy is professionally coached self-change.** Therapy can be a useful step in the change process, but at some point the client has to do the heavy lifting alone.

After years of research, Dr. Prochaska and his colleagues identified six well-defined stages of change in all successful self-changers:

1. Precontemplation
2. Contemplation
3. Preparation
4. Action
5. Maintenance
6. Termination

The key to successful change is in knowing where you are in the change process and applying the right technique. You must be ready.

We'll talk more about the six stages of change in just a moment. You'll learn how to identify where you stand and what tools you should apply. First, get familiar with the nine techniques used by people who've successfully changed their behavior. As you read through them, remember that they bring success only when they are applied at the right time in the overall change process.

The Nine Tools for Change

Consciousness Raising.   This is about awareness. You need to be aware that a certain belief or behavior exists. It's also about becoming aware of the ways in which you use your defenses, resistance, and "mental tricks" to maintain a certain belief or behavior. You've already done work in raising your level of consciousness surrounding your beliefs and behaviors about money in the previous chapters. That will allow you to better use this technique when it's time to apply it.

Social Liberation. This involves finding external environments where you have more choices and alternatives for your desired behavior. No-smoking areas, for example, provide an alternative for smokers. Investment clubs can provide people who have an aversion to investing with a social environment and the support they need to make different choices in this area of their finances.

Emotional Arousal. This is similar to consciousness raising, but it works on a deeper level. You may be aware of a spending problem, for example, but that awareness moves to a different level when you realize you don't have the money to cover the cost of your child's tuition.

Self-Reevaluation. This involves reappraising your problem and thinking about how your life will be once you've conquered it. During this type of reevaluation you can really see and believe that your life will be better without the behavior you want to change. The pros outweigh the cons as well as the costs of what you have to give up.

Commitment. This is an acknowledgment that you are the only one who can act on your behalf—you willingly accept responsibility for the change you want to make and what it will take to make it. The first step involves telling yourself you are ready for change. The second involves going public and telling others that you have made a firm decision to change. Public commitments can be very powerful and effective when it comes to changing behavior!

Countering. This involves substituting healthy responses for unhealthy one. You could go to the movies instead of the mall, for example, when your tendency to spend yourself out of a bad mood creeps up. The key is to keep trying until you find countering behaviors that work.

Environment Control. There are some similarities to the social liberation and countering techniques in environment control. In environment control, however, you actively restructure your environment so that the probability of the problem-causing behavior's occurring is reduced. Leaving your credit card at home would be an example of controlling your environment, as would having a portion of your salary automatically deposited into an investment account.

Reward. This involves things like self-praise or getting yourself a present when you reach a certain goal. These things can be under your control, or the control of others. A friend with whom you've shared your desire to put $1,000 into an emergency fund might take you to a movie when you reach that goal, for example. One thing to watch out for is that many of us do not believe that we have to right to be rewarded when we change or modify a behavior, yet we believe that we deserve to be punished when we fall short of our goals. Dr. Prochaska and his colleagues discovered that punishment is rarely used by successful self-changers.

Helping Relationships. This involves getting care and support from significant people in your life. Many of us have trouble admitting when we need help, so we limit our opportunities for assistance. In addition, many of the people we care about may be uncomfortable hearing that we're in trouble. They may find it difficult to provide the support we're looking for. It's important to identify the people who can provide the type of support that you need when you employ this technique.

Determining Where You Stand

It's important to read through all of the information about the various stages of change so that you can identify which stage you're in. Once you've made that determination, do the exercises in the section about your particular stage, so that you can learn how to apply those techniques that will allow you to move on. If you can't decide where you stand, do the exercises in all the sections you think might apply to your situation. This will help you gain clarity.

The Six Stages of Change

The Precontemplation Stage of Change

The first stage of change is called *precontemplation*. People in this stage usually have no intention of changing their behavior. Few in this stage think they have a problem at all. Precontemplation is characterized by resistance, excuses, rationalizations, and denial.

Precontemplators rarely want to change themselves, just the people and circumstances around them. If people around you have been trying to get you to change your lifestyle or certain behaviors, like losing weight, quitting smoking, or eliminating debt, but you think the problem is with them and not you, you're probably in precontemplation! Movement out of this stage is often unintentional.

"Precontemplators are likely to stay stuck in this stage unless one of two things happens: A crisis occurs, or an event like becoming a parent, turning 50, or some other milestone—situations where your environment no longer supports your lifestyle," Dr. Prochaska told me.

Defense Mechanisms for Precontemplators.   Precontemplators are often demoralized, feeling like a situation is their fate. They don't want to think or talk about their problem because they feel the situation is hopeless. These feelings of inevitable failure protect them from trying to change. They give up on themselves, and accept one or more of what Dr. Prochaska and his colleagues have identified as the *Four Self-Change Myths*.

> *Myth 1: Self-change is simple.* It's simply not! We shouldn't become embarrassed or frustrated by our struggles, or feel bad if someone tells us they had an easier time making a change than we did.
>
> *Myth 2: It just takes willpower.* Willpower doesn't really come into play until you're ready to take action. As Dr. Prochaska says, it can seem reasonable to conclude that you don't have enough willpower if you fail to make a desired change. But failure to change when relying on willpower alone really means that willpower alone was not enough!
>
> *Myth 3: I've tried everything; nothing works.* This goes back to timing—making sure that you've used the right process, at the right time, in your change effort.
>
> *Myth 4: People don't really change.* Dr. Prochaska and his colleagues have blown this myth out of the water, by interviewing countless numbers of successful self-changers. We've all changed. Look at a picture of yourself 10 years ago. Now look in the mirror. Think about how your attitudes, beliefs, and behaviors have also changed over the past decade. Change happens in all of us, whether we want it to or not.

Precontemplation or Lifestyle Choice?   It can be difficult to identi-fy whether you are a precontemplator or you're simply living the life of your choosing. Some people truly believe, for example, that they are okay with debt and overspending. Dr. Prochaska says the follow-ing three questions can help distinguish between problem behavior and lifestyle choices:

1. **Do you discuss your behavior pattern?** Precontemplators are usually defensive. They tend to tell people to mind their own business. They tend to see feedback as an attempt to control them, rather than a sign of caring. They use their defense mechanisms to avoid an issue.
2. **Are you well informed about your behavior?** Precontempla-tors tend to avoid learning about their problems. If they see an article or television show about getting out of debt, they would likely turn the page or channel.
3. **Are you willing to take responsibility for the consequences of your behavior?** Precontemplators don't enjoy thinking about the consequences of their actions. Ask them to think about how a behavior will play out 5, 10, or 15 years down the road, and they are likely to become defensive and avoid answering the question.

Successful Change Techniques for Precontemplators.   Dr. Prochaska found that precontemplators use three change techniques to move out of this stage: consciousness raising, helping relationships, and social liberation.

Consciousness Raising.   You've done a lot of this in the early chapters in this book. Did you discover anything about your beliefs and atti-tudes, when we looked at your various "scripts" that might be a tool for resisting change? In addition, think about some of the defense mech-anisms precontemplators use. Do you see them in your behavior?

_____

_____

_____

_____

Helping Relationships.   Our defenses rarely fool others. Think about someone who cares about you and will "call you out on your stuff!" This person should not rush you toward action before you are ready, but they should help you come up with different ways to look at your problem. Precontemplators rarely change without outside assistance. Think about the people who could help you. List their names below, and the ways in which you think they can provide support. They may need your guidance.

_____

_____

_____

_____

_____

Social Liberation.   Self-help groups, like investment clubs and women's investing groups, are great examples of resources for precontemplators. In addition, precontemplators should plan social outings that don't include spending a lot of money—a trip to the museum, for example, rather than a trip to the mall. Your ability to enjoy non-financially destructive behavior will do wonders for your self-esteem. Identify social liberation techniques that will support your desired changes. Write them down and determine ways to incorporate them into your lifestyle. Don't forget to enlist the helping hand(s) that you identified as a helping relationship.

_____

_____

_____

_____

_____

The Contemplation Stage of Change

As a person moves from the precontemplation stage to the contemplation stage, he or she starts to seriously consider making a change. Awareness is developed during contemplation—awareness of the consequences of various actions and awareness of the benefits of change.

Contemplators want to change, but this stage is also character-ized by resistance, due in large part to a fear of failure. They are also fearful of losing some, or all, of their identity. "I've been a shopa-holic all of my life. If I give that up, what will I do with my friends on the weekends?"

These fears tend to bring out the procrastinator in the contem-plator. In fact, many chronic contemplators substitute thinking for acting. Conflicts and problems hang suspended. Decisions are never finalized. Some in this stage seem to be waiting for some kind of divine intervention to come along and change them.

Contemplators are not ready to prepare for action until they achieve greater understanding of their behavior. This is a positive aspect of the stage. Dr. Prochaska says jumping into action while you're in this stage will almost surely lead to failure.

Defense Mechanisms for Contemplators.   Dr. Prochaska and his colleagues have identified these common traps that contemplators can fall into:

- *The search for absolute certainty.* People who are stuck in con-templation may tend to spend their time analyzing, think-ing, and worrying, instead of taking action. Some people, for example, will spend decades in therapy, exploring every aspect of various issues, without taking actual steps to change their situation. They seem to harbor the belief that if they get enough information, change will be easy or the problem will go away.
- *Waiting for the magic moment.* Someday, I'll save money. Some-day, I'll quit smoking. Someday, I'll get out of this unhealthy relationship. Most of us are familiar with the concept of waiting for the perfect time for change. It's driven by a belief that there will be a magic moment when change will just happen or, at least, be easy. When the kids grow up. When things slow down. Things, of course, never slow down.
- *Wishful thinking.* It's much easier to wish for change than to work toward it. The problem is that wishing rarely works. "I wish that I could max out my credit cards and never have financial trouble." "I wish that I could spend $60,000 for a car and still save enough to start my own business." Any of these sound familiar? Have these kinds of wishes ever made desire a reality?

- *Premature action.* Trying to take an action before you're ready can serve as a conscious or an unconscious way out. Dr. Prochaska is quick to point out that a period of contemplation prior to taking action is *essential* for lasting change. Premature action can also come as a result of being nagged or threatened by an outside party. When failure comes, the contemplator can now say, "See, I tried. I knew I couldn't do it. Get off my back." Now they can justify putting off future attempts to change.

Successful Change Techniques for Contemplators.   Dr. Prochaska and his colleagues found that contemplators use four change techniques to move out of this stage: emotional arousal, consciousness raising, self-reevaluation, and helping relationships.

Emotional Arousal.   As we discussed, emotional arousal happens on a deeper level than simply becoming aware of your problem behavior and its consequences. Losing a business, a job, or a relationship over financial issues; an illness; or other life-changing events can provide the kind of emotional charge that is needed to make the decision to change a behavior.

Dr. Prochaska says we can also emotionally arouse ourselves. He says movies that focus on our specific problem are wonderful ways to rouse emotions. He cites Jack Lemmon's portrayal of an alcoholic in the movie *Save the Tiger* as a motivating event for many alcoholics. Creating your own stimulus can also be helpful. Overweight people, for example, may want to use mirrors to encourage them to change. Have your partner secretly record one of your conversations about money. Then listen to the things you say. These can be effective tools.

Your imagination can be a great tool as well. Think about your problem behavior and imagine the distressing scenarios it could lead to. Think about the people it is affecting and the consequences to your lifestyle. Imagine how this behavior will play out 5, 10, or 20 years down the road.

Write down some ways in which you can use the emotional arousal technique.

_____

_____

_____

_____

_____

Consciousness Raising. If you're in the contemplation stage of change, you're probably more open to hearing information about your problem than someone still in precontemplation. Use this as an opportunity to gather information that can motivate you to change your behavior. Reacquaint yourself with the goals we identified in Chapter 3.

Come up with questions that will raise your level of consciousness about your problem, such as:

- What do my finances have to look like in order for me to retire in 10 years?
- How long will it take me to pay off my credit card debt if I pay only the minimum?
- What are my triggers for overspending?
- What am I thinking and feeling before I make a purchase that works against my goals?

Paula will help you learn to ask the right questions and find the right answers for specific financial situations in Part II. For now, take a look at your goals. Come up with some solid fact-finding questions and start looking for the answers!

_____

_____

_____

_____

_____

Self-Reevaluation. Take the information you learned about a behavior and its consequences through consciousness raising and put some well-informed thought into how you'll feel if you continue to act in the same way. How will I feel about myself if I continue to stick my head in the sand when it comes to estate planning? How will I feel about not having enough money to help my child pay for college? In addition to asking the "tough questions," Dr. Prochaska and his colleagues noticed that contemplators getting ready to move out of this stage begin to think before they act. Pausing and thinking before you make a purchase or a financial decision can do wonders for your financial stability.

Contemplators also create a new self-image for themselves. "If I move past that behavior, how will I feel? How will others think of me? What types of things will I be saying and doing?" They begin to act according to their new image. Contemplators also make a decision to take action, sooner rather than later, after weighing the consequences of change to themselves and others around them.

Take some notes on how you'll feel if you continue the financial behaviors you want to change. Think about the consequences. Think about how you'd re-create yourself by discarding that behavior, and when you'd like to begin to make changes.

Helping Relationships. Contemplators benefit a great deal from empathy—someone who's able to see his or her perspective. Unconditional support and warmth is also critical during the contemplation phase. No insults, threats, "I told you so," or false praise. Dr. Prochaska says it's wise to remember that "warmth begets warmth." The best way to ignite warmth and compassion from your helpers is to extend it. Helpers can also offer assistance with gathering information that could be helpful during self-reevaluation and consciousness raising.

Think about the best people to help you move out of the contemplation stage of change.

The Preparation Stage of Change

People in this stage are usually planning to take action within the next month and are making the necessary adjustments before they begin to change their behavior.

"They are preparing for how hard taking action is really going to be. They are creating a plan to deal with the expected and unexpected challenges that are to come, because their realization of the benefits of change have gone up," Dr. Prochaska told me.

Preparation is the cornerstone of effective action. When it comes to financial behavior, preparation could include things like setting up accounts to have money automatically allocated toward your goals: a savings account to beef up emergency funds or an account to save for your child's college education, for example.

In this stage, the focus has shifted to what life will be like once you have changed your behavior. Dr. Prochaska gives the example of a therapy group for people addicted to cocaine. Those who were in the contemplation stage delighted in talking about their war stories—the crazy things they did to get cocaine, the crazy things it did to them. This was appropriate because they were still in the decision-making stage. Those in the preparation stage found these stories to be distracting. They talked about how their lives and relationships would change for the better without cocaine.

Dr. Prochaska and his colleagues found that people who rushed into action without preparation usually failed to make the changes they desired.

Successful Change Techniques for Those in the Preparation Stage. People in the preparation stage use three techniques to move forward: self-reevaluation, helping relationships, and commitment.

Self-Reevaluation.   Using self-reevaluation to create a new image absent your destructive behavior will help you let go of the past. Ask yourself: What is my potential if I change? What will it free me up to become? How will my life be enhanced? This type of forward-looking self-inquiry allows people in this stage to turn away from old behavior. It can be scary and downright hard to let go of habits and patterns, but "your new self will be there to greet you." In addition, people in the preparation stage can use self-reevaluation to help them make change a priority. As you plan for your life without the financial behaviors you want to change, what do you need to do? Cut up your credit cards? Set up automatic payments for certain accounts? Learn more about investing?

Write down the ways in which you will prepare for change, and put these things at the top of your "to do" list. Also, list the benefits those changes will bring to your life.

_____

_____

_____

Helping Relationships.   The preparation stage usually involves noticeable changes that may affect the people around you. If you haven't enlisted their help, this is a good time to do so. In addition, it can be quite tempting and easy to give up in the first days and weeks of your new behaviors. You may need the support of helping relationships now more than ever.

Dr. Prochaska says it's important to let people know the best ways to help you. Tell them, for example:

- "Don't keep asking how I'm doing."
- "Lend a helping hand when you see that I'm overwhelmed."
- "Tell me how proud you are that I'm doing this."

Who are the best people to help you out of the preparation stage? What tips will you give them when it comes to helping support you in your change effort?

_____

_____

_____

_____

_____

Commitment.   While commitment involves a willingness to act and focus on the ways in which you want to change, the spark that really ignites its force is your belief in your ability to change. Believing in how you've assessed yourself and your problem during self-reevaluation will help build your will and your confidence. Still, Dr. Prochaska says, at some point you're just going to have to make tough choices when you are committed to change, and throw yourself into a new way of behaving. Even the strongest commitment and intention, however, can be overwhelmed by fear of failure. There are no guarantees that change will be successful. Dr. Prochaska says we must learn to accept the anxiety that comes with this fear. He offers these five commitment techniques to help combat that stress:

1. *Take small steps.* Gathering the emotional and physical supplies you need to prepare for action should not be underestimated or rushed. Cut up your credit cards, for example, before you take more aggressive steps to get out of debt.

2. *Set a date.* Choosing a date can help prevent premature action and prolonged procrastination. The date should be realistic, but as soon as possible, so that you can capitalize on the momentum you've built to make this change.

3. *Go public.* Going public with your intended change not only enlists the support of people who care about you, but also gives you a fear of embarrassment if you fail. Both can be a major motivator when it comes to staying committed.

4. *Prepare for a major operation.* If you were having a major operation, you would plan for it and your recovery. Do the same for the behavior you want to overcome. Put the "surgery" first. That means your relationships, moods, and other areas of your life will change accordingly. Also, plan to take as much time as you need to recover, just as you would after a physical surgery.

5. *Create your own plan of action.* Knowing yourself and what works for you is critical when it comes to creating a *specific* plan of action. Your plan should list a variety of techniques for coping with expected barriers. Spending one day a month versus one day a week with your neighbor who pushes the "keep up with the Gateses" button, for example. Reviewing your previous attempts to change may also hold valuable information about your barriers.

Create a plan of action to change financial behaviors that work against your goals and values. Set a date, and list small steps you can take as you move toward your new behavior.

_____

_____

_____

_____

_____

The Action Stage of Change

When you are prepared to make the changes you desire, and you've planned for them, action can come naturally. You're committed and you're motivated. Now you can act on that debt repayment plan. Taking action also involves making the difficult changes in your life that will allow you to alter your behavior. This could mean avoiding certain places and people or getting rid of things in your everyday environment so that you can stay focused. Being aware of the pitfalls during this stage greatly improves your chances for success. Dr. Prochaska and his colleagues identified these four danger zones:

1. *Taking preparation too lightly.* More often than not, action without preparation will not last for very long. Without the necessary preparation and plan for temptation, the inclination to return to the problem behavior is too strong.
2. *Cheap change.* Change requires work, effort, enormous energy, and standing up to the efforts by others to hold onto the old you. Your best friend may try to talk you back into your old spending patterns to assuage her own guilt. Standing up to this pressure is extremely difficult, but there's nothing cheap or easy about change.
3. *The myth of the magic bullet.* Many of us believe that there is one magic way to bring about successful change. Dr. Prochaska says some people are attracted to his work because they believe it provides some miracle cure. Relying on a single technique will likely lead to failure. Try different techniques in different doses until you find one that works for you.
4. *More of the same.* Many of us have a tendency to cling to old techniques that are bringing partial success or no success at all. By holding onto old methods, we don't allow room for change, and we don't give ourselves opportunities to recognize that other, perhaps better, techniques and variations exist. Combining a variety of techniques at the right time is the best way to get your desired results.

Successful Change Techniques for People in the Action Stage. Dr. Prochaska and his colleagues found that people who successfully moved through the action stage of change used four techniques: countering, environmental control, rewards, and helping relationships.

Countering.   This involves finding a healthy substitute for the behaviors you want to change. This eliminates much of the risk of the old habits returning.

I once interviewed Dr. Bernard Arons about behavior substitutions for people with addictions. Dr. Arons is the executive director and CEO of the National Development and Research Institutes, which does scientific research on substance abuse and other health concerns. He has served in a number of positions, including mental health and substance abuse adviser to Tipper Gore during the Clinton administration in the early 1990s. During our interview, he pointed out that when we engage in a behavior that we know is self-sabotaging (e.g., reckless spending), we experience some form of gratification. Perhaps shopping gives a sense of control to someone who feels that his or her life is in chaos. He says it is important to find an alternative nondestructive way to achieve that same affect. This can be very helpful when it comes to finding effective countering techniques.

Dr. Prochaska and his colleagues identify these effective countering techniques:

- *Active diversion.* Keep busy. Find an activity to preclude problem behavior. This could be anything—reading a book, calling a friend, walking, having sex—anything that refocuses your energy.
- *Exercise.* This is one of the most beneficial substitutes for problem behavior. Dr. Prochaska says omitting exercise from a self-change plan is like fighting a foe with one hand tied behind your back. Exercise prepares you mentally and physically for change and reduces your stress levels.
- *Relaxation.* Research has shown that 10 to 20 minutes of daily deep relaxation can bring lasting improvement to your physical and mental health. You will experience an increase in energy, which is needed to take action. Decreased anxiety, improved sleep, and improved concentration are other positive effects. Yoga, meditation, prayer, and progressive muscle relaxation (systematically relaxing every part of your body) are some of the relaxation techniques successful self-changers use.
- *Counterthinking.* We've had much discussion about the importance of "rewriting your scripts" in the previous chapters in this section. Counterthinking is quick, takes little energy, and can be used anytime, anywhere. When a negative thought is getting the better of you, give it a reality check. What are you

telling yourself that's making you so upset? Is it the truth? Are there more rational assessments of the situation? Absolutes are a good indication that you should come up with a new thought: "I must buy this car," "I am bad at saving money"—anything that doesn't leave room for discussion. What new tune are you going to play when that old song comes up? How are you going to rewrite scripts that don't serve your best interests? We discussed this in Chapter 6.

- *Assertiveness.* Trying to overcome problem behavior can result in feelings of weakness and helplessness, especially if there are people or other outside influences that resist or are threatened by the changes you want to make. Exercising your right to be heard can build confidence. In addition, don't forget your right to make mistakes, change your mind, and resist other people's judgments, as well as your right to not have to justify yourself. Assertion crosses the line into aggression, however, when your assertiveness comes at the expense of others.

Think about some of the financial behaviors you want to change. Think about what it is in that behavior that you find gratifying. A sense of control? A distraction from boredom or depression? Come up with some countering techniques for your behavior. Be specific about how and when you can apply them. Don't forget that you'll probably have to be flexible and try new techniques until you find the right solution.

_____

_____

_____

_____

_____

Environmental Control. While countering involves changing your responses, environmental control involves changing the situation itself. It involves changing your environment in a way that reduces temptation. An alcoholic, for example, has a better chance of success if he doesn't keep alcohol in his house. Controlling your environment is not a sign that you are too weak to be tempted. It shows that you are strong enough to put yourself in the best possible situation to achieve success.

While avoidance is very effective when it comes to controlling your behavior, it's not always a permanent solution. Other techniques Dr. Prochaska and his colleagues suggest include:

- *Cues.* Eventually you will be faced with a cue that triggers your problem behavior. I once met a woman who felt the need to go on a shopping spree and get a makeover every time she saw well-dressed celebrities on award shows like the Oscars. Dr. Prochaska recommends using your imagination to confront and plan for cues. Perhaps this woman could conjure up that anxious feeling she gets from watching the award shows. She could remind herself that her family and friends love her for who she is, not for what she wears, until the feeling subsides. She could also tell one of her friends she has identified as a helping relationship that she will plan to call them for a "pat on the back" when the Golden Globe Awards come on.
- *Reminders.* Reminders are very effective during the action stage. Putting a picture of your dream house where you keep your credit card, for example, will stop you from rushing full steam ahead into a purchase that is not high on your priority list. "To do" lists are also effective. Put your countering techniques near the top—things like counterthinking, Relaxing, and Exercise.

Think of some adjustments you can make to your environment that will be helpful to your change process. Think about ways in which you can avoid situations that will trigger your cues. Come up with a plan to deal with those inevitable temptations. In addition, come up with ways in which you can remind yourself to stay on track.

_____

_____

_____

_____

_____

Rewards. Many people do not believe they should be rewarded for changing problem behavior. Failing to reinforce positive self-change efforts, however, is essentially punishing yourself. Many psychologists say that punishment only temporarily suppresses troubled behavior.

Dr. Prochaska and his colleagues found that successful changers rewarded and praised themselves for their efforts. Many used these three techniques:

1. *Covert management.* If you choose to take a deep breath and relax until the urge to spend passes, congratulate yourself. Telling yourself, "Nice job, it feels good to be in control," is a much more effective tool for change than beating yourself up for having the urge in the first place. The latter breaks down self-esteem, whereas a "pat on the back" reinforces your effort and makes you feel good about the success you're having in the change process.

2. *Contracting.* Many successful changers make contracts with themselves during the action stage. Written contracts are even more powerful than spoken ones. "Every time I put $200 into my child's college fund, I will take the two of us to the movies." Tapping into helping relationships when using this technique can make your contracts binding.

3. *Shaping up.* By this Dr. Prochaska and his colleagues mean taking small steps to gradually reshape your behavior. Well-practiced, well-rewarded moves to put $25 a month into an investment account, for example, can lay a strong foundation for the time when you want to make the larger investments needed to attain your goals. Gradually reshaping your behavior builds your resolve.

What are some of the ways you can reward yourself for your change efforts? Make a contract with yourself or with someone you've identified as a helping relationship. Think of small steps you can take to lay the foundation for bigger changes.

_____

_____

_____

_____

_____

Helping Relationships. You'll rely on your helping relationships more in the action stage than you have in the previous stages. It's important that your helpers are clear on your intentions, and the kind of support you need from them. You should ask for their help with your countering techniques. You could ask a friend to exercise with you, and ask him or her to help you change your environment so that you can avoid tempting cues. As we discussed earlier, helping relationships are also very useful when it comes to sticking to contracts. In addition, praise and reward from those close to you goes a long way in helping you feel good about the changes you've made.

Think of the best people to provide you with the support you need during the action stage of change. Who will help you with the ways in which you are trying to counter your behavior? Who will help you stick to your contract? How can they be of the most help? Write their names down, and let these people know you need their help.

_____

_____

_____

_____

_____

The Maintenance Stage of Change

Successful change is not measured by action alone. It means you must sustain your new behavior for years, decades, or a lifetime. Sound challenging? It is. In addition, you won't get that confidence boost from seeing the immediate results of taking action or the praise from people who see your dramatic changes. The new you is old news. Dr. Prochaska and his colleagues define the maintenance stage as a busy, active period of change that requires you to learn new coping methods. They say sustained, long-term effort and a revised lifestyle are the key ingredients to successfully maintaining the changes in your behavior.

As we discussed, there was something about your problem behavior that brought you some kind of gratification. That attraction will still be there long after the habit is broken. It is important to acknowledge that you are still vulnerable to the problem, even though you see it has no value.

Dr. Prochaska and his group identified three common threats to successfully maintaining your new behavior:

1. *Social pressures.* These come from those around you. They may engage in the behavior you're trying to change without realizing their actions are having an impact on you.
2. *Internal challenges.* These usually result from overconfidence or other forms of defective thinking. "I've been able to stop using my credit card for six months. This one purchase won't make a difference."
3. *Special situations.* The desire to "keep away from the Joneses and Gateses" and not buy cars that take up 30 percent of your income might be greatly challenged if you get a big bonus.

It is difficult to prepare for these challenges because they are usually unexpected. Daily temptation and self-blame when urges or relapses hit were prevalent in people who failed to make lasting change.

Successful Change Techniques for People in the Maintenance Stage. People who successfully maintained behavioral change continued to use the change techniques that worked for them. These brought them success:

Commitment. Once you've changed your lifestyle and moved into maintenance, the threats to your new behavior are fewer and far between. You've controlled your environment, developed countering measures, and enlisted support. That can make it easy to become complacent. Watch for signs like these that show that you have lessened your commitment: "I'll skip my credit card payment just this month," "I'll start saving again next month; I already know that I can." Also, always remember to be patient with yourself, and keep your eye on the long-term benefits of your change.

Reward. Take credit and responsibility for your accomplishments. Remembering how far you've come and praising yourself for it can help keep you connected to how much you've already committed yourself. This can be a great motivator when it comes to sustaining that commitment.

Helping Relationships. Give your helper permission to confront you if you start reverting to old behavior, express overconfidence, expose yourself to tempting situations, or break your contracts. Also, let your helper know that he or she is "on call."

Dr. Prochaska suggests making a crisis card for your wallet or pocketbook that also includes a set of instructions to follow if you slip:

1. Review the problem.
2. Substitute positive for negative thinking.
3. Remember the benefits of change.
4. Engage in rigorous distraction or exercise.
5. Call my helper. Being a helper to someone with a similar problem is also helpful during the maintenance stage.

Environment Controls.   Environment controls are also a key ingredient when it comes to successfully maintaining change. As your confidence grows, you'll become more comfortable in the presence of certain temptations, but you may not be totally immune to them. Continue to avoid people, places, and things that could compromise your change efforts, especially in the early months of maintenance.

Countering.   Dr. Prochaska says that working to create alternative behaviors is one of the most important parts of maintenance. Make time for something that you've always wanted to do. Countering negative thinking is equally as important. Plan time to step back, check your thinking, and give yourself a reality check, so that you can keep negative thoughts from gaining a foothold.

Think about some of the things that could challenge your long-term efforts to sustain change. Maybe it's your environment? Maybe things or situations trigger you to spend in ways that don't serve your interests? Deeply embedded scripts? What techniques will you use to counter these challenges? How will you maintain your commitment over the long term?

_____

_____

_____

_____

_____

The Termination Stage of Change

Termination is the final stage of change. There is a great deal of debate over whether a behavior is ever truly terminated, or if people spend their lives in the maintenance stage. Age seems to be a factor. The older we get, the more likely we are to simply lose our appetite for some of our old behaviors. Dr. Prochaska and his colleagues did find that some tendencies and behaviors could be terminated. They identified these four criteria in people who had changed their behavior for good:

1. *A new self-image.* If a major revision in your attitude and self-image takes place during maintenance, there is a good change you will reach termination.
2. *No temptation in any situation.* People who reached the termination stage felt no temptation to return to their old behavior, regardless of the situation. It wasn't even a thought.
3. *Solid self-efficacy.* People who move from recovering to recovered are convinced that they can function well without ever engaging in their former behavior, no matter what the situation. This is not false bravado; it's a genuine self-confidence. Their focus is on themselves, not their problems.
4. *A healthier lifestyle.* People modify parts of their lives during maintenance. They control their environment, change their social contacts, and counter old behaviors with new healthier ones. When a behavior is terminated, a healthier lifestyle becomes their way of life, without struggle.

Imagine yourself once you've terminated the behavior you want to change. How will you think, feel, and act? How will your thoughts be different? How will your lifestyle be different?

_____

_____

_____

_____

_____

Use your notes as we put together "Your Story." Identify the changes you want to make, where you are in the change process, and the techniques you will use to move forward. "Your Story" will serve as a point of reference when you identify specific financial behaviors you need to change in Part II.

Again, many thanks to Dr. Prochaska and his colleagues for their groundbreaking work on the science of change. I hope it helps you make the changes you desire a reality.

Your Story

In today's broadcast: The story of a person who understands the benefits of making a change.

(Your name) realized that in order to make *his/her* goals a reality, the following changes had to take place in *his/her* financial behavior:

_____

_____

_____

_____

_____

Those behaviors are the result of the following scripts and beliefs:

_____

_____

_____

_____

_____

(Your name) is in the_____ stage of change when it comes to getting rid of the financial behavior(s) that work against *his/her* best interests. *He/She* will use the following techniques to move out of that stage (e.g., environmental control: He will cut up his credit cards; helping relationship: His best friend Sam will take him to the movies when he saves $1,000):

_____

_____

_____

_____

_____

(Your name) also needs to keep tendencies to use the following defense mechanisms in check:

_____

_____

_____

_____

_____

We here at the station applaud *(your name's)* efforts in making the changes to _his/her_ financial behavior that will make _his/her_ most important dreams become a reality!

Moving Forward

Keep tabs on where you are in the change process when it comes to the specific changes Paula asks you to make to your financial behavior in Part II. That way, you can apply the techniques that will bring your desired results.

Also, don't forget to try different variations of the change techniques until you find something that works.

Congratulations on completing the challenging work that you've been asked to do Part I! You are now ready to look at your finances with a new perspective that will allow you to channel your financial resources toward your most important goals.

PART II

THE NUMBERS

"If one advances confidently in the direction of his dreams, and endeavors to live the life which he has imagined, he will meet with success unexpected in common hours."

—Henry David Thoreau

CHAPTER 10

Your Bottom Line

In the past few chapters, Stacey has been helping you to define the life you really want. You've identified the internal resources you have to make those goals a reality, and you've identified any beliefs and behaviors that may be standing in your way. In the coming chapters, you will learn how to use your finances in a way that makes that life possible.

Unfortunately, for most of us, our finances tell tales of people making spending decisions that don't necessarily reflect who we really are or what's really important to us.

In Part II, you're going to learn how to change that. We will create a plan that integrates your goals, finances, and your "financial personality" (the stuff you learned about yourself in Part I).

In order to get the numbers side of your story, we need to determine what you're worth, what you owe, and what you spend. We must also identify your spending that is the result of scripts, or beliefs and behaviors, that don't serve your best interests. We're going to put a dollar figure on those expenses, and reallocate that money toward your most important goals.

Your Bottom Line

We will be working from a chart, which we'll call your Bottom Line, throughout Part II of this book. It will serve as the road map for all your future financial decisions.

As you've learned, there is much more to your financial choices than dollars and cents. This is reflected in your Bottom Line. We've

Table 10.1   A View of John's Bottom Line

		Scripts	Change Process	Technique	$ Adjustment	After
Clothing	$400	SS, IS	P	SR, HR, C	($200)	$200
Personal savings	$200	SS, IS	P	SR, HR, C	$200	$400

made space for you to account for the beliefs that drive your choices, where you stand in changing those that don't serve you, and the steps you'll take to make those changes. We think having to literally face your values and your barriers each time you look at your finances will be an important factor in keeping your financial decisions aligned with your priorities.

Here's how your Bottom Line will serve as the blueprint for all of your financial choices, and make you account for any parts of your financial personality that may be working against your higher inter-est. Take a look at Table 10.1, which shows a part of a Bottom Line we created for someone we'll call John.

John determined that he needed to save $200 more a month to achieve his goal of starting his own business when he retires. He reexamined his expenses, and decided that he could cut the spend-ing he and his family used for clothing each month in half. He and his wife decided that making their children pay for some of their clothes would teach them a valuable lesson about money. They suc-cessfully made their case, and he reallocated that money toward his personal goal.

There was a lot more to that change in John's finances than just dollars and cents. He realized in Part I that societal pressures to "keep up" and be the strong "male provider" played a role in the spending he did on clothes, so it was important for him to keep those tenden-cies in his awareness.

John was in the preparation stage of change. That meant self-reevaluation, commitment, and the helping relationships of his friends and family would allow him to move into the action stage.

Now take a look at the spreadsheet that you'll be working from in Table 10.2, so that you can become familiar with it.

Table 10.2   Your Bottom Line

Goals	Net Worth
1	
2	
3	
4	Income
5	

Money Going Out				
Before				After
	Scripts	Change Process	Technique	$ Adjustment

Savings:				**Savings:**
Goals:				Goals:
Personal				Personal
Family				Family
Big picture				Big picture
Legacy				Legacy
Material				Material
Emergency fund				Emergency fund
Retirement				Retirement
Education				Education
Investments				Investments
Expenses:				**Expenses:**
Allowances				Allowances
Charity				Charity
Child care				Child care
Clothing				Clothing
Education				Education
Food				Food
Gifts				Gifts
Hobbies				Hobbies
Housing				Housing
Maintenance				Maintenance
Medical				Medical
Miscellaneous				Miscellaneous
Self-care				Self-care
Taxes				Taxes
Transportation				Transportation
Travel				Travel
Utilities				Utilities

(continued)

Table 10.2 *(continued)*

Insurance:		Insurance:
Health		Health
Long-term care		Long-term care
Disability		Disability
Home		Home
Auto		Auto
Other		Other
Debt payments:		Debt payments:
Credit card		Credit card
Personal loans		Personal loans
Total Expenses:	**Total:**	**Total Expenses:**
Total Income:		**Total Income:**
Difference		**Difference**

What's Your Bottom Line?

Let's take a moment and discuss how this chart should be filled in.

You'll see a space at the top for your top five goals. Review what you've identified to be your top priorities in Chapter 3. Go ahead and fill them in.

You'll also see a place for your income at the bottom of the chart. We'll use your monthly gross figure, because we'll be looking at your expenses on a monthly basis. Go ahead and fill it in.

We'll determine your net worth in the next section.

We also want to highlight any of the family scripts, societal scripts, or internal scripts (those songs that go off in your head) you've identified, that may be at work in your finances. When the time comes, in that "Scripts" column, you will put:

- "FS" next to those expenses where you see family scripts at work
- "SS" where you see societal scripts at work
- "IS" where you see internal scripts at work

In addition, you've learned to identify where you are in the change process laid out by Dr. Joseph Prochaska, Dr. John Norcross, and Dr. Carlo DiClemente in Chapter 9. In the column of your Bottom Line labeled "Change Process," you will note which stage you're in, when we get to an area of your finances that you want to change. You may realize, for example, that you are in the contemplation stage of changing your investment behavior.

Here is the list of the six stages of change as identified by Drs. Prochaska, Norcross, and DiClemente. You will use the abbreviations in parentheses when you fill in the chart.

1. Precontemplation (PC)
2. Contemplation (C)
3. Preparation (P)
4. Action (A)
5. Maintenance (M)
6. Termination (T)

You also learned about the nine techniques that successful self-changers use when it comes to change. You will write the techniques that apply to your stage in the "Change Technique" column. You can use the following abbreviations:

• Consciousness raising (CR)
• Social liberation (SL)
• Emotional arousal (EA)
• Self-reevaluation (SR)
• Commitment (C)
• Countering (CT)
• Environment control (EC)
• Reward (R)
• Helping relationships (HR)

You came up with the specific ways in which you will use those techniques in Chapter 9. You will review those, and apply them as we move through this part of your financial planning.

Now, let's figure out your net worth.

Where You Are Now: Your Net Worth

Your net worth tells you where your hard work has brought you to financially. It's a snapshot of your financial position at this point in your life. Why do one? Because you have to know where you are now to begin the journey to where you want to go.

Let's figure out your net worth, so that we can plug it into your Bottom Line.

Your net worth is your total assets (what you own), minus your total liabilities (what you owe). We'll use Table 10.3 to help you figure out your number.

Table 10.3   Net Worth Statement (as of xx/xx/xxxx)

Assets	Amount
Liquid Assets:	
Cash	
Checking	
CDs	
Savings	
Other liquid assets	
Total liquid assets	
Investment Assets:	
Stocks	
Bonds	
Mutual funds	
Other investment assets	
Total investment assets	
Retirement Assets:	
401(k)	
403(b)	
IRA	
Other retirement assets	
Total retirement assets	
Personal Assets:	
Primary residence	
Other real estate	
Automobiles	
Market value, other vehicles	
Jewelry	
Collectibles	
Other personal assets	
Total personal assets	
TOTAL ASSETS	_____

Liabilities	
Current Liabilities:	
Credit card debt	
Lines of credit	
Taxes due	
Other current liabilities	
Total current liabilities	

Long-Term Liabilities:
Mortgage balance
Automobile loan
Education loans
Other long-term liabilities
    Total long-term liabilities

TOTAL LIABILITIES   _____

NET WORTH (Assets – Liabilities)   _____

What's It Worth?

In order to figure out what your assets are worth, think of what they would bring you if you sold them today. Maybe your car cost you $20,000 five years ago, but it won't be worth that today, unless it's some kind of antique. The same principle applies to your furniture.

Used-car Web sites like Edmunds.com can help you determine the current value of your car. EBay and other Web sites can help you figure out how much other household items are worth. It's best to get a professional estimate of assets like jewelry, furs, and collectibles. That will not only help you with your net worth statement, but also with estate planning and insurance.

So tally it all up—anything of value you have. Those are your assets. Subtract your mortgages, loans, credit card debt, and any other amounts of money you owe. Now you have your net worth. Put it down in your Bottom Line.

What Do You Think?

Take a look at that number. Is it surprising in any way? If so, how? Many people expect to have a higher net worth than the numbers reflect. All you need to remember is that you only need to have enough assets to support the lifestyle you desire. That tends to be a lot less than people expect, once they eliminate all of the spending that is inconsistent with who they really are and what they really want.

Remember, this is just a starting point. From now on, you'll be doing things differently. Once you start to live in a way that reflects what's really important to you, your numbers will look very different.

Spending: Where's It All Going?
Where Should It Be Going?

The ways in which you adjust your spending will help determine the amount of money you have to channel toward your goals. In this section, you will learn how to identify your spending patterns. You want to see clearly how the unnecessary ones are taking resources away from your priorities. You'll also identify money that can be reallocated toward the things that are important to you, and you'll learn how to reflect all of this on your Bottom Line.

There is a broad section on your Bottom Line called "Money Going Out." You'll notice it's divided into two parts: "Before" and "After." On the left side of the sheet, the "Before" side, we will fill in where your spending stands now, so that we have a reference point for the changes that will help you reach your goals.

We think it's helpful for people to look at their finances on a monthly basis. Many of us pay bills on a monthly schedule. Some of your expenses, like taxes, for example, may not occur on a monthly basis. Divide those annual costs by 12, so that we can fit them into this monthly picture of your finances.

Take a moment and acquaint yourself with the savings and expenses categories on the left side of the chart. Here are some guidelines.

- **Savings**. We'll be discussing what you should be saving toward your goals throughout this entire section of the book. We'll also go into more detail on the other parts of your life that need to be supported by savings in an upcoming chapter. Retirement and investing get their own chapters as well.
- **Allowances** means discretionary money put aside for adults, single or married, as well as children.
- **Charity** includes anything you donate to various organizations, and the regular dues or tithe you may pay at your place of worship.
- **Child care** includes day care, night care, nannies, and babysitting.
- **Clothing** is for clothes and shoes.
- **Education** covers college tuition, private school, tutoring, or any other education expenses your child incurs.
- **Food** includes groceries, school lunches, and eating out.

- We want you to guesstimate what you spend on **Gifts** for things like holidays and birthdays each year. It's smart to budget for these items. The holiday season can blindside a bank account or credit card balance!
- **Hobbies** can include things like cooking classes and tennis lessons.
- **Housing** includes mortgage, rent, and property taxes.
- The **Maintenance** column refers to maintenance and repair costs for your home and other assets like your car, stereo, or computer.
- **Medical** includes out-of-pocket costs for doctor, dental visits, and prescriptions.
- You may have other expenses that we didn't make allowances for; put those in the **Miscellaneous** column.
- **Self-care** includes things like haircuts, manicures, massages, and gym memberships.
- **Taxes** include federal, state, and local taxes. If not included in your mortgage payment, your real estate taxes should also go here.
- **Transportation** includes your car payments, parking, and gasoline.
- **Travel** includes anything from a weekend road trip to a European holiday.
- **Utilities** include electricity, heat, water, phone, cable, and Internet access costs.
- We will fill in your **Insurance** expenses when we get to the chapter on insurance.
- **Debt** refers to credit card debt and personal loans, like student loans (anything besides mortgages and auto loans). We will fill in the debt portion of the chart when we get to the chapter on debt.

The Next Seven Days—How to Create a History of Your Spending

Unless you've just inherited a billion dollars or won the lottery, your means are limited. There's only one way to make your finances work for you. You need to figure out how to allocate your money to support what's really important to you. A history of how you spent your money in the past can help.

If my clients are having spending issues, I always ask them to track their money. That's because in order to reallocate money, we have to know where it's going now.

How to Track Your Spending

You can do this in several ways. Take your pick:

- *Charge it.* Charge absolutely everything on your credit cards. Then you get a nice record at the end of every month with all your expenses on it. A caution here: Since it's easier to spend credit than cash, the result just might take your breath away.
- *Check it out.* Write checks for everything. You will have a record, as you did for your credit cards. There may be less pain, since you presumably will not spend money you don't have.
- *Receipts anonymous.* Ask for receipts for everything. At the end of the week, spread them out on the dining room table and figure out what you spent.
- *Buy the Book.* Buy a little book and write everything down.

Also add in typical expenses that may not have shown up in the week you're tracking.

Why do you need a system? Because money disappears. Can you recall to the penny how you spent the last $100 you took out of the ATM? Even financial planners have a tough time remembering.

Ideally, tracking your spending will become a habit. I urge you to continue to do this for a least a month, so that you get an even clearer picture of your spending patterns. But for now, let's keep it to a week.

One Week Later ...

Now that you've kept track of your spending, use what you've learned to fill out the expenses on the "Before" side of your Bottom Line. Some of your expenses may not have come up during this week, and things like travel may not occur monthly. Figure out how much needs to be set aside each month to pay for irregular expenses. Again, we're creating a monthly picture of your finances.

But before we make any adjustments, we're going to put your spending through a reality check (see Table 10.4).

Table 10.4   Your Spending

Savings:

Goals:
Personal
Family
Big picture
Legacy
Material
Emergency fund
Retirement
Education
Investments

Expenses:

Allowances
Charity
Child care
Education
Food
Gifts
Hobbies
Housing
Maintenance
Medical
Miscellaneous
Self-care
Taxes
Transportation
Travel
Utilities

Insurance:
Health
Long-term care
Disability
Home
Auto
Other

Debt Payments:
Credit card
Personal loans

Reality Check

You've kept track of your expenses for a week.

1. At first glance, what do you think of your spending? Which items do you look at and say, "Yes, that was absolutely worth it"? Which ones do you look at and not even remember buying? Take a moment and identify those expenditures that you know right off the bat you can eliminate or reduce. Put the amount you can save in the "$ Adjustment" column.

2. Take a look at "Your Story" at the end of Chapters 4, 5, and 6. Notice the things you said about the ways in which you would like to be living, and how your finances have to look to support those goals. Do you see any spending that would be different or eliminated if you were living your ideal life? Reconsider those expenses, and put the amount you can save in the "$ Adjustment" column.

3. As you look at "Your Stories," also notice the ways in which family, societal, and internal scripts affect your spending choices. As you look at your spending, do you see any expenditures that are the result of that scripting? Put FS, SS, or IS in the scripts column next to those expenses. Reconsider those expenses, and put the amount you can save in the "$ Adjustment" column.

4. In Chapter 5, you learned how to calculate how many hours of work it takes to pay for your various expenses. I won't ask you to make this determination for each of your expenses, but look at them through that lens. Do you see expenditures that are just not worth the amount of time it takes to pay for them? Figure out how much you can reduce them, or if you can eliminate them all together, and put that amount in the "$ Adjustment" column.

5. Now, look through your expenses again, and ask yourself the following four questions:

   - Was this item in keeping with my goals?
   - Was this item in line with my values?
   - Did I have the money to pay for it?
   - If I answered "no" to any of the above questions, was there something in my past experience that caused me to spend this way?

What are the items you think you can eliminate completely? Do you see any expenses you can reduce by 75 percent? 50 percent? 25 percent? Identify those expenses, figure out how much you think you can reduce them, and write those amounts in the "$ Adjustment" column.

6. You've identified the ways in which you want to adjust your spending, and you've noted the scripting that was behind that old behavior. In order to make those changes a reality, you need to be clear on where you are in the change process, and which techniques you need to apply. Fill in those columns on your Bottom Line.

7. Identify the spending adjustments that will be easy to make. Make them. When it comes to items that require more effort, like getting rid of a car, or changing your housing situation, for example, think about where you stand in the change process when it comes to aligning your spending with your values. What do you need to do to get yourself ready for action? Apply those change techniques, and set a realistic time frame (sooner rather than later) to make the big adjustments.

More Money for Your Goals

Total the amounts you identified in the "$ Adjustment" column. This is money that can now support things that are really important to you. And we haven't even looked at the big components of your financial life! For now, hold off on reallocating that money until we look at those other areas of your finances.

Before we move on, see if any of the following tips can help you reduce your immediate spending even more.

- Eat out less, particularly at work.
  - Buy fewer prepared foods. Instead, involve your family in planning for and preparing meals.
- Reduce clothing expenditures.
  - Let's say that you currently spend $200 a month on clothes. But when you look in your closets, you realize that you don't need any more clothes for at least a year. So take that $200, and put it in a place that more truly reflects your ideal life. Maybe it's retirement. Maybe it's charity. Maybe it's college for the kids.

- ◆ Shopping at auction and discount Web sites like eBay and Overstock.com can also save you a bundle. Many brick-and-mortar retailers also offer discounts for shopping on their Web sites.
- Look at transportation expenses.
  - ◆ Could you live with cheaper cars, one car, or no car? I work in Manhattan and know many people who spend $500 a month on parking. Some of these folks use their cars only a few weekends a month. Renting a car when they needed it would save them a bundle!
  - ◆ Also see if there are times when you can use public transportation. You may even be able to incorporate a little reading time or time for listening to music.
- Cut down on utility costs.
  - ◆ Maybe you don't need a landline. Perhaps your cell phone or Internet phone will do for all your calling needs. See if your utility company charges you less if you wash your clothes at off hours.

CHAPTER 11

Saving Money

Personal saving as a percentage of disposable personal income was a negative 0.8 percent in March 2007, according to the U.S. Bureau of Economic Analysis. This is the lowest level of any industrialized nation.

How does that happen in the wealthiest nation in the world? There are many theories out there, but one theme that seems consistent throughout is that we are an incredibly materialistic society. We tend to measure success by our possessions. Stacey and I think that there are so many pressures out there to "keep up," as you saw in Chapter 5, that living beyond our means has become a way of life for many of us. Savings have become an acceptable loss in the battle to make ends meet, and those "ends" cost a lot more than they used to!

Believe me, we're not judging anyone. These pressures are drummed into us from such an early age from the media, our peer groups, and our communities that it's a wonder we don't completely lose sight of our values. In this chapter, we're going to make sure that the ways in which you save money reflect your core beliefs.

Why It's Important to Save

Let's start by calling a savings account what it really is—insurance. It's insurance that you can continue to live the lifestyle of your choice in the future, and honor your goals and dreams. Perhaps you want to see the world, start a business one day, or send your child to college. Savings also protects the life you've worked so hard to create if something unexpected occurs. Nothing can derail a life plan faster than an event like a job loss.

Your Savings, from the Inside Out!

As you can see, savings are a necessary part of an overall spending plan, not something you do *after* you spend. Think about some of the things you learned about yourself in Part I with Stacey. What do you think of your saving habits? Is this an area of your finances you decided you want to change?

Take a look at "Your Story" at the end of Chapter 4. Do you see any ways in which the lessons you learned when you were young are affecting your saving habits? What do you think of those lessons now? What are the thoughts and behaviors you'll adapt to transcend those early messages if they don't serve you? How can you build on them if they are consistent with your values? Take some notes if it will help you gain clarity on this issue. Also put FS (for family scripts) in the "Scripts" column in the "Savings" row of your Bottom Line if your early messages are having an impact on your savings habits.

_____

_____

_____

_____

_____

Let's do the same thing with societal messages. Look at "Your Story" at the end of Chapter 5 to see if you identified social pressures like "keeping up with the Joneses," gender scripts, or scripts about your race or ethnic group that are affecting the way you save money. Take some notes if it helps you clarify these influences. Also put SS (for societal scripts) in the "Scripts" column in the "Savings" row of your Bottom Line if social pressures are at work in your savings.

_____

_____

_____

_____

_____

Stacey had you listen to the song the "voices in your head" sing when you think about saving money. What tune does it sing? Do those messages serve you? Jot them down, and note some songs and behaviors that will drown out those old tunes! If the perception you have about your saving ability plays out in your financial behavior, put IS (for internal script) in the "Scripts" column in the "Savings" row of your Bottom Line.

_____

_____

_____

_____

_____

If you've decided to change your savings habits, where do you think you are in the change process that you worked on in Chapter 9? Again, here are the six stages Dr. Prochaska and his colleagues identified, and the abbreviations you should use on your Bottom Line, as you put that information onto the chart:

1. Precontemplation (PC)
2. Contemplation (C)
3. Preparation (P)
4. Action (A)
5. Maintenance (M)
6. Termination (T)

Review the techniques that will allow you to move out of that stage. Also, look at the notes you made on how you can make that technique work best for you. You may want to jot some of those down, so that you can refer to them during this chapter. In addition, use the following abbreviations to note those change techniques in the "Technique" column on your Bottom Line:

- Consciousness raising (CR)
- Social liberation (SL)

- Emotional arousal (EA)
- Self-reevaluation (SR)
- Commitment (C)
- Countering (CT)
- Environment control (EC)
- Reward (R)
- Helping relationships (HR)

_____

_____

_____

_____

Saving for Your Goals

Let's put your goals right at the top of your saving priorities. Other typical savings goals are:

- Building an emergency fund
- Retirement
- College for the kids
- Paying off debt

Those last three get their own chapters.

As for your goals, we need to figure out how much you need to save. List the five goals you identified in Chapter 3, and let's figure out how much you'll need to save to achieve them in today's dollars. In a moment, I'll show you how to determine what these things will cost in the future.

Let's say that one of your personal goals is to spend a month in Australia. Some quick research on the Internet can help you figure out how much this will cost in U.S. dollars. A search on Google took me about five minutes to figure out that that my "dream month" would cost about US$4,000.

I found a two-bedroom apartment for US$2,000, airfare for US$900, and I figured about US$1,000 for expenses. Of course, bargain shopping and things like house swapping could greatly reduce that cost, but you get the idea.

List your goals and your best guesstimate of what they would cost today in the following chart:

Personal Goals	Cost
Family Goals (Don't panic if education goals make this number skyrocket. We'll address this in an upcoming chapter.)	
Big Picture Goals	
Legacy Goals	
Material Goals	

There are two things you need to keep in mind when it comes to saving for the future. First, a dollar tomorrow is worth less than a dollar today, because of inflation. Second, if you have long-term goals, you can put the power of compounding to work for you.

Table 11.1   Impact of Inflation on Goals

| Amount Today | What It Would Be in | | |
	5	10	20 years at 3% Inflation
$20,000	$23,185	$26,878	$36,122
50,000	57,964	67,196	90,306
100,000	115,927	134,392	180,611
200,000	231,855	268,783	361,222
500,000	579,637	671,958	903,056

Here's how inflation works: Let's say you need $50,000 for something in the future. You need to calculate what $50,000 will cost when you need it. Table 11.1 calculates it out, assuming 3 percent annual inflation. So $50,000 will "cost" about $67,196 ten years from now. Use this chart as a guideline.

The next question is: How much do you need to save to reach those goals? If we can get you a 7 percent rate of return on your money, which we'll discuss in Chapter 15, you'd need to save about $386 per month to have $67,196 ($50,000 adjusted for inflation) in 10 years. You'd have to put away $172 per month to have $90,306 (the same $50,000 adjusted for inflation) 20 years from now (see Table 11.2, and use it as a guideline).

There are two things going on in this example. One is how much inflation increases the amount you need, especially over very long periods of time. The second is how the power of compounding (how interest builds on itself over time) can help you build your savings.

Table 11.2   What It Would Cost per Month to Save for These Amounts at 3 Percent Inflation and 7 Percent (Tax-Deferred) Return

	5 Years	10 Years	20 Years
$20,000	$322	$154	$69
50,000	805	386	172
100,000	1,610	772	345
200,000	3,220	1,544	689
500,000	8,049	3,860	1,724

What should you be saving each month in order to achieve your goals?

Use these tables as a guide to determine what you'll need to save to meet your goals in your desired time frame:

	Monthly Savings
Personal Goals:	
Family Goals:	
Big Picture Goals:	
Legacy Goals:	
Material Goals:	

What do you think when you see what your goals will actually cost? Many people look at the numbers and think there's no way they'll be able to meet their savings targets. It all depends on the changes you are willing to make in your life to make your dreams a reality. That's why we had you reconnect with your real values on things like the car you drive, the neighborhood you live in, and the other expensive assets that are using up your resources. You may want to consider making some big changes.

Your goals are worth achieving. Stacey calls our deep dreams and desires the *tools* our minds and hearts use to tell us what will make us really happy. As we're both fond of saying: "This is no dress rehearsal; this is real life." Happiness should be non-negotiable!

Think about the changes you need to make to make your dreams a reality. Keep referring the process laid out by Dr. Prochaska and his colleagues to see where you really stand in the change process, and those proven techniques they've identified that successful self-changers used to move forward. Also think about the scripts and behaviors that may be holding you back and how they would have to change if you were living your ideal life.

As we move through the following chapters, you will see even more ways in which you can adjust your finances, so that you have more resources for your priorities.

Time Horizon

Time horizon is the amount of time you have until you actually need to cash in your investments and use the money.

- If you have less than 1 year, you will want to keep your money in cash equivalents—money market accounts, savings, and short-term CDs.
- If your time horizon is 1 to 5 years, most of your money should be in cash and short-term bonds.
- If your time horizon is 5 to 10 years, your money should be in cash, bonds, and perhaps some equity (stocks).
- If your time horizon is 10 years or more, you want a mix of stocks, bonds, and cash. The farther away your goal is, the more money you should have in stocks, depending on your risk tolerance.

Building an Emergency Fund

In addition to thinking of the money you save for your goals as necessary expenses, I want you to think of an emergency fund in the same way. Expect the unexpected. The main reason to save for emergencies is so that you won't be knocked completely off course by life's little surprises like a job layoff, a breakdown in your car, or even a broken sink. Many people are forced to turn to their credit cards in the event of an emergency—a move that puts even more distance between them and their goals.

You know your financial obligations better than anyone, but a general rule of thumb is that you should put aside the bare minimum you would need to live on for three months if your income stopped. Look at your monthly expenses, and multiply them by three.

Do your current emergency savings fall short? If so, by how much? How much would you have to save each month to get this emergency fund up to par in three months? Six months? One year?

How about allocating another 25 percent of the money you came up with when you reexamined your expenses to your emergency fund until it's big enough to allow you to live without income for five or six months?

These numbers may change when you look at the other parts of your financial life, but leave them as a placeholder for now.

If you don't have a savings account, open one at the institution where you do the bulk of your financial transactions. Many will give you perks if you have more than one account with them. If possible, set up a system to have money automatically deducted from your paycheck each month to ensure that your emergency fund is a priority.

Tips on Saving

Again, we're going to look at the different aspects of your financial life, and align them with your priorities. That will free up all of the money you are spending on things that are not that important to you. There are steps you can take in your day-to-day life that will also help you save even more. I've seen the following tips work wonders.

20 Savings Tips

1. Carry cash only. If you don't have credit cards with you, you can't spend money you don't have.
2. Take your lunch. You can pack a good lunch for $1 or $2 using homemade ingredients. In New York, where I work, a sandwich and a soda can run $7. Saving $5 on lunch 100 days a year is $500 you didn't have before.
3. Share your things. If you have good relations with your neighbors, divvy up what you buy for your house and yard. Every house does not need its own rototiller or snowblower. Every house doesn't even need its own lawnmower.
4. Try starting a neighborhood work group. Each month, take on a project in each other's houses—saves money, builds community.
5. Save fancy coffee shops for special occasions. Use the coffee or tea supplied by your employer or bring your own from home.
6. Not everything that says "dry clean" really has to be. Start with your sweaters. Wash at home in cold water with special detergent made for that purpose.
7. Set your heater one degree colder and your air conditioner one degree warmer than it is now. Saves money and energy.
8. Clean with simple, reusable ingredients like soap and water and rags, rather than expensive chemicals and disposable cloths. Saves money and the environment.
9. Do it yourself. Are you paying for someone to clean your house while you pay to go to a gym to work out? Power vacuuming can be a great workout!
10. Make your errands more time and energy efficient. Park in a central location and walk around town—saves gas and time and is good exercise.

11. Stop buying your children things because all their friends have them. If they are obsessed with a certain item, help them figure out how to buy it themselves. Your children are not going to die because they do not have the latest-model iPod.

12. Make sure you have the correct amount withheld from your paycheck for federal and state taxes. Many people have too much withheld. It's not a good idea—you are making an interest-free loan to the government. Put the extra money from your paycheck into savings instead and earn interest.

13. Bank your refunds and rebates. When you get a check, put it directly into your savings account.

14. Avoid fees for bounced checks. Keep a close watch on your checking account or look into overdraft protection.

15. Collect your change in a big jar. Add a dollar bill now and then. When the jar is full, take it to the bank.

16. Have you just paid off a loan? Continue "paying" it by putting the same amount of money into savings.

17. Sign up for automatic bill payment if your bank offers it at no cost. Paying 10 bills monthly through the mail costs $3.90 per month or $468 per year.

18. Go without buying clothes for six months. Most adult Americans have way too many clothes.

19. If you are paid biweekly, budget as if you are paid twice a month and put those two "extra" paychecks per year right into savings.

20. Save off the top. Nothing works better than direct deposit into a savings account. If you don't see it, you are much less likely to spend it.

Try some of these! In addition, pay attention to any resistance you're feeling to the changes you want to make to your savings. Continue to work with those change techniques.

Your Bottom Line

Savings should be as much a part of your daily thinking as spending. Make savings a priority, and you will rest easier at night. Once you've determined the amounts you need to save, determine how it affects your monthly budget, and insert that number into your Bottom Line.

CHAPTER 12

Debt

WIPE THE SLATE CLEAN

Nothing can derail a financial plan quite as effectively as debt. It is a tremendous drain on the resources—financial, psychological, and emotional—that should be working to make your dream life a reality.

We're all familiar with the scary realities of debt. Still, the average American household has racked up between $7,000 and $9,000 in credit card debt, depending on who is doing the calculating.

Credit card companies are eager to help you bury your head in the sand. They bombard you with offers to raise your credit limits, shift balances, and the like. Some will even send you checks to lend you money to pay off your loan!

Stacey and I know many people who have tried to budget their way out of credit card debt and failed. Planners often complain that they help clients get out of debt only to see them fall back into the debt trap over and over again. Look at the statistics. High debt levels are the norm in our society. Something is clearly not working when it comes to helping people fix this problem.

We think the problem lies in the fact that few people see debt for what it really is: a spending problem. There are few things in life that work as simply as money. Don't spend more than you have.

Debt is a great example of the duality of human nature. We know it's bad for us, but we do it anyway.

When you think about your finances, it's easy to determine if your debt levels are a problem. Just be honest with yourself. You and Stacey looked at some of the messages and scripts that may explain why your spending behavior needs to change. Do any of these sound familiar?

- "I was so good last week. I can charge a few things this week."
- "I deserve this."
- "What's the use? I'll never get out of debt at this rate. I might as well enjoy myself."
- "I've had a really bad day and I need a treat to cheer my-self up."
- "One day, I'll have a big payday. That's when I'll pay off my debt."
- "My spouse/mother/father/brother/sister/best friend will give me money if I get into too much debt trouble."
- "I don't know how to budget. No one ever taught me."

We'll look at your own messages in a bit. But before we go any further, let's identify your debt.

Your Debt Load

I've made two columns. In the left column, list the items you would consider to be "good" debts. Some examples may include a mort-gage, a student loan, or a loan to start a business. On the right side, do the same for those items you consider to be "bad" debts. While personal loans for things that are not important to the lifestyle you desire can be examples of bad debt, it is primarily incurred through credit cards. List the monthly payments you make to all of your cred-itors. List interest rates and balances as well.

Good Debt	Bad Debt
Creditor:	**Creditor:**
Monthly payment:	Monthly payment:
Balance:	Balance:
Interest rate:	Interest rate:

Creditor:
Monthly payment:
Balance:
Interest rate:

Creditor:
Monthly payment:
Balance:
Interest rate:

Creditor:
Monthly payment:
Balance:
Interest rate:

Creditor:
Monthly payment:
Balance:
Interest rate:

Creditor:
Monthly payment:
Balance:
Interest rate:

Creditor:
Monthly payment:
Balance:
Interest rate:

Total:

Total:

Your Ideal Relationship with Debt

Write down your goals for your debt. For example, you may want to be debt free in five years, except for the mortgage on your house.

_____

_____

_____

_____

_____

Now, let's look at any scripts and messages that may be standing in your way. We'll begin with lessons you learned from your family's attitudes and behaviors regarding debt.

They may be positive—your parents may have never had credit card debt. They could also be negative. One of your role models might have thought that debt was "the American way." Take a look at "Your Story" at the end of Chapter 4. Were there lessons that are contributing to your debt? If nothing jumps out, take a moment and think about this. Write some notes about those early lessons that are contributing to any "bad debt" you may have incurred. Also, put FS (family script) in the designated column of your Bottom Line.

_____

_____

_____

_____

Let's do the same thing with societal messages. Look at "Your Story" at the end of Chapter 5. Are social pressures to "keep up with the Joneses," follow gender scripts, or follow scripts regarding your race or ethnic group affecting your debt levels? If so, write them down. Also put in SS (societal script) in the designated column of your Bottom Line, so that you can red-flag these tendencies when they challenge your spending and saving decisions.

_____

_____

_____

_____

What about those songs playing in your head? Did you notice any in the list of common excuses earlier in the chapter? Look at "Your Story" at the end of Chapter 6. Is there anything that is working against your higher interests when it comes to debt? Are there any messages that are helping you live your ideal relationship with debt? Either way, write them down. Also put in IS (internal script) in the designated column of your Bottom Line.

_____

_____

_____

_____

When you look at where you would like to be when it comes to your debt versus where you are, what has to change? Where do you think you are in the change process when it comes to this behavior? Again, here are the six stages Dr. Prochaska and his colleagues identified, and the abbreviations you should use on your Bottom Line. Note your status in the "Change Process" column.

1. Precontemplation (PC)
2. Contemplation (C)
3. Preparation (P)
4. Action (A)
5. Maintenance (M)
6. Termination (T)

Review the techniques that will allow you to move out of that stage. Also, look at the ways in which you decided to make that technique work for you, and begin to apply them, if you haven't already. In addition, use the following abbreviations to note those change techniques in the "Technique" column on your Bottom Line:

- Consciousness raising (CR)
- Social liberation (SL)
- Emotional arousal (EA)
- Self-reevaluation (SR)
- Commitment (C)
- Countering (CT)
- Environment control (EC)
- Reward (R)
- Helping relationships (HR)

_____

_____

_____

_____

_____

Getting Rid of Your Debt

Stacey and I believe that paying off your debt should be one of your top priorities. Use the following guidelines to help you determine how much of your savings you should allocate toward debt reduction. We're going to reduce your debt, while being mindful of your other objectives.

If your "bad debt" is more than 50% of your annual income . . .

Pay off "bad debt"	Emergency money (3 to 6 months of expenses)	Retirement	Other goals
70%	10%	10%	10%

If your "bad debt" is between 25% and 50% of your annual income . . .

Pay off "bad debt"	Emergency money (3 to 6 months of expenses)	Retirement	Other goals
60%	10%	20%	10%

If your "bad debt" is between 1% and 25% of your annual income . . .

Pay off "bad debt"	Emergency money (3 to 6 months of expenses)	Retirement	Other goals
50%	10%	25%	15%

If you don't have any "bad debt" . . .

Pay off "bad debt"	Emergency money (3 to 6 months of expenses)	Retirement	Other goals
0%	25%	45%	30%

Once your bad debts are paid off and your emergency money is funded . . .

Pay off "bad debt"	Emergency money (3 to 6 months of expenses)	Retirement	Other goals
0%	0%	60%	40%

Go to http://cgi.money.cnn.com/tools/debtplanner/debtplanner.jsp and calculate how long it would take to pay down your debt using those allocations.

If you don't like what you see, go back and put your expenses through another reality check. Don't cut out so many things that you're going to feel deprived. If you do, it's unlikely you'll stick to the plan.

Make sure you add these amounts to your Bottom Line.

As you work with your numbers, here are some specific steps that will help you reduce, and eventually get rid of, your debt bills.

How to Get Rid of Those Pesky Credit Card Bills

What does credit card debt cost? That depends on the interest rate, and those rates are generally very high. If you have $20,000 in credit card debt at 25 percent annual interest, then the interest alone costs more than $400 per month. So if you are making a payment of $400 per month, you aren't even paying the principal! You will *never* pay the debt off. (In fact, it will continue to grow.) If you pay $500 per month, you will pay the debt off in about seven years. And in addition to the $20,000 in principal, you will have paid about $23,000 in interest.

That's why people like Stacey and me keep nagging you to get rid of your credit card debt. No one can afford to pay $23,000 in interest on a $20,000 debt.

If credit cards are a problem, we have a solution . . .

Stop Using Credit Cards.   When I tell this to people in workshops, they typically react as if I'd shot them. How can a person exist in our society without credit cards? Strangely enough, most stores still take cash. There are a lot of studies that indicate that we spend less when we buy with cash. That's important. **We are more in touch with our spending when we use cash**.

Think about the last expensive item of clothing you bought. What would you have done if you had not had credit cards with you? Would you have made a special trip to the ATM to get the money to buy the item? Or would you have just not bought it?

Stacey and I don't want you to deprive yourself of anything—except fear and worry. But we also want to make sure that the things you buy are of significance to you. Using only cash will make that task easier. You won't just be whipping out a credit card without thinking. When you carry cash, you tend to ask yourself: "Do I need this? Is this important?"

If you absolutely need something other than cash—if you travel extensively, for example—use a debit card rather than cash.

It's a radical move in today's world, when everything is electronic. But the people who pay off their debt fastest have stopped using credit cards.

The following strategies will also help:

- Decide that this is a priority.
- Start building up your emergency fund by putting aside at least $1,000. That way, you won't have to go into debt again every time something goes wrong.
- Understand your spending priorities.
- Make sure you pay at least the minimum on every credit card each month ON TIME!
- Pay more than the minimum using one of two strategies:
  1. Highest interest card first (you'll pay less money in the long run).
  2. Lowest balance card first (it's very satisfying to pay off a debt in full, no matter how small).

Many people find it helpful to keep track of their debt payoffs. You can use a spreadsheet or a pencil and paper. Note how much you are paying off each month. Tracking your progress helps you see that you are moving in the right direction.

There are lots of books and Web sites that will tell you to consolidate your debt by moving to a new credit card, by taking out a home equity loan, or by calling your creditors and asking for a lower interest rate. But unless you are disciplined, this method will backfire. You'll feel a sense of relief, which could prompt you to start overspending again. The problem will get worse instead of better.

That's why we recommend paying off your credit card debt just the way it is. That way you will know what you have and what you owe and you will not be lured into a false sense of security.

If You Think You Need Help . . .   Sometimes, it's just too hard to do it yourself. You need outside help. Credit counseling may be able to provide it.

Stacey and I think the best route to go when it comes to credit counseling agencies is with a nonprofit organization. Why take on more expenses if you're already having a problem?

One nonprofit we are familiar with is the National Foundation for Credit Counseling (NFCC). To find an agency affiliated with NFCC near you, call toll-free, (800) 388-2227, or go to www.nfcc.org. You can also write to them at:

National Foundation for Credit Counseling
801 Roeder Road, Suite 900
Silver Spring, MD 20910

You can expect your credit counselor to contact your creditors. He or she may be able to get your interest rates lowered. You will also receive a debt-management program, which includes a realistic repayment plan and an overall budget.

We'll also discuss how to find planners who practice mindful money management in Part III. If you decide you want go this route, they will also be able to help you create a debt repayment plan.

When Debt Is an Addiction

Sometimes debt is just a bad habit. People get into debt because they stop keeping track of what they are spending, and it builds up without their noticing. Sometimes it's because of a cataclysmic financial event. But it can also be the result of an addiction to spending, as real and as dangerous as an addiction to cocaine.

Are you one of those people? The following quiz comes from the Debtors Anonymous Web site (www.debtorsanonymous.org):

15 Questions*

Most compulsive debtors will answer "yes" to at least 8 of the following 15 questions:

1. Are your debts making your home life unhappy?
2. Does the pressure of your debts distract you from your daily work?
3. Are your debts affecting your reputation?
4. Do your debts cause you to think less of yourself?
5. Have you ever given false information in order to obtain credit?

*The "15 Questions" are reprinted with permission of Debtors Anonymous General Service Board, Inc. (DAGSB) Permission to reprint the "15 Questions" does not mean that DAGSB necessarily agrees with the views expressed herein. DA is a program of recovery from compulsive debting only. Use of DA materials in connection with programs and activities which address other problems, or in any other non-DA context, does not imply otherwise. Copyright 2007 Debtors Anonymous General Service Board, Inc.

6. Have you ever made unrealistic promises to your creditors?
7. Does the pressure of your debts make you careless with the welfare of your family?
8. Do you ever fear that your employer, family or friends will learn the extent of your total indebtedness?
9. When faced with a difficult financial situation, does the prospect of borrowing give you an inordinate feeling of relief?
10. Does the pressure of your debts cause you to have difficulty sleeping?
11. Has the pressure of your debts ever caused you to consider getting drunk?
12. Have you ever borrowed money without giving adequate consideration to the rate of interest you are required to pay?
13. Do you usually expect a negative response when you are subject to a credit investigation?
14. Have you ever developed a strict regimen for paying off your debts, only to break it under pressure?
15. Do you justify your debts by telling yourself that you are superior to the "other" people, and when you get your "break" you'll be out of debt overnight?

Why Your Debt Level Matters

In addition to your overall financial and emotional well-being, one of the main reasons we're putting so much effort into controlling your spending and debt patterns is that they impact your credit history.

Think about the significance of your credit history. We take on credit to purchase some of the most significant things in our lives: a home, an education, a business. Our credit histories also show how seriously we take paying our bills and how we feel about carrying debt.

Creditors, potential insurers, potential employers, and even medical establishments use our credit histories to formulate opinions about our characters, and to determine the likelihood that we will be responsible when it comes to meeting payment obligations.

Make sure your credit history is accurate. There is only one Web site providing free annual credit reports under federal law: www.annualcreditreport.com" (*Source:* www.ftc.gov). There are other Web sites that look and feel like this one, but this is the real deal.

Once you get your credit report, take a close look at it. Make sure that the information is correct. When I took a look at mine recently, one of my past addresses was listed as New York City. I have never lived in New York City, though I work there. So I called and had that address removed. Was this an attempt at identity theft? It might well have been.

Check and see that all of your payments have been recorded correctly. Are there delinquencies? Are there problems? If there are, you are entitled to dispute them. To dispute information, you can either do it online or call the credit reporting company during normal business hours.

Mistakes are so common on credit reports that I'm going to ask you right now to commit to checking yours once a year. Make a note on your calendar, in your PDA, or anyplace that will help you remember to do this.

Your Credit Score

Credit rating agencies use your credit history and a complex formula to calculate your credit score.

Your score is composed of several factors. The most important is your bill-paying history. Therefore, if you're consistently late when it comes to paying bills, if you have accounts that have been sent to collection, or if you declare bankruptcy, there will be big, negative consequences for your credit score.

Outstanding debt is a close second, with consideration given to how much you owe on mortgages, car loans, home equity, and your credit cards.

The total amount of credit you have outstanding may also be a factor. If you have five credit cards, each with a $10,000 credit limit, you have $50,000 in available credit. If a creditor believes that $50,000 is the most you can pay, he or she may be unwilling to extend more credit.

The length of your credit history is also factored in. In this case, the longer the better. Even if you've decided to consolidate the number of credit cards you have, consider holding onto the one you've held the longest. And since closing accounts may have a negative impact on your score as well, you may simply want to cut up cards you no longer use.

Your mix of credit is also a component. Lenders like to see a rich variety: credit cards, mortgages, car loans, and so on, to show that you are good with money.

Finally, the amount of times you apply for credit is considered in the formula to calculate your credit score. This part of the equation does, however, make adjustments for people who are shopping for car loans or mortgages.

Not only do lenders use your credit score to determine whether or not they will give you credit, but they also use it to determine the rate they will charge you on everything from mortgages and car loans to auto insurance.

The scores range from 300 to 850. The higher the number, the better you look to lenders. People with higher numbers get the lowest interest rates. A score below 500 is generally considered a high risk, while a score of 720 or higher will get you the best rates. Most of us have scores between 600 and 800. The higher your score, the lower the rates you pay on consumer loans and mortgages.

Auto Loans and Leases

Which makes more sense, an auto loan or a lease? The real answer is that neither makes sense. A car is a depreciating asset—its value goes down every month. Any planner will tell you that it does not make sense to finance a depreciating asset. Why borrow money to pay for something that will be worth less tomorrow than it is today?

Stacey and I do want you to spend money for things that are important to you. If cars are your abiding passion and your one regret in life is that you did not become an automotive engineer, then it makes sense to put aside more money than normal for your car. But if you want to buy a fancy car just to make yourself feel good, ask yourself: How good will a large car payment make me feel? Am I doing this for me or for how I will look to others? And how important is that really?

If cars are not a major passion of yours, then it makes sense to look at the numbers. If you crunch the numbers, your best bet is to pay cash for as good a used car as you can afford.

If you must use credit to buy a car, then normally you get the best deal by buying a used car when there is a low interest rate offered on a loan. Lease payment options look very attractive, but it's not very economical to have a new car every three or four years. Unless driving a late-model car is one of the things that are truly important to you personally or professionally, there are probably better ways to spend your money.

One leasing option Stacey and I think makes sense is taking over a lease someone else had and thought better about. The benefits to you are no down payment and a short-term lease. There are dozens of Web sites that will arrange this transaction. Type "take over a car lease" into Google, and you will get more than a million hits.

Mortgages and Home Equity Loans
and Lines of Credit

A mortgage is a cheap way to borrow money. If you have a 6 percent mortgage and are in the 25 percent federal marginal tax bracket, your mortgage costs you only 4.5 percent net of taxes.

Taking out a home equity loan or line of credit to pay off your credit card debt may sound like it makes smart financial sense when you compare that low mortgage rate to the 19 percent with no tax deduction you pay for your credit card, right? Wrong!

Do you really want to pay off your credit cards over as much as 30 years? Do you want to still be paying for that pair of shoes you bought on sale at Saks after you've retired? Any planner will tell you that it's not wise to pay for short-term items with long-term money.

Instead of focusing on how to pay less in the short term, think about the long-term benefits of paying off your mortgage as soon as possible. Jonathan Clements wrote an interesting article about this in the *Wall Street Journal.* If we don't pay our mortgages off before we retire, most of us will be pulling money out of savings to make mortgage payments. This will have the effect of increasing our taxable income and therefore our taxes. The additional taxes will most likely offset any tax advantages you'd get from the mortgage. At retirement, it makes sense for most people to have their houses paid off.

What kind of mortgage should you have? There are lots of fancy mortgages on the market right now. Many of them have low initial interest rates, but with interest-only mortgages, for example, none of your payment is going toward the principal. If the value of your house does not go up, you would have been better off renting.

All of these fancy mortgages have a date when monies are due and adjustments trigger. If you're not prepared, the results can be disastrous. Remember all of the news stories about people whose financial lives were devastated because their subprime mortgages were adjusted upward in early 2007? Unless you are sure you will have moved by the time some of these triggers kick in, or you have a crystal ball that tells you exactly where interest rates are headed, forget about these types of mortgages.

Financial planners like 15- and 30-year fixed mortgages. Thirty-year mortgages give you the lowest payment, and you can always turn them into a 15-year mortgage by adding principal to the payment. (Do not pay for one of those additional principal payment programs.

If you do not have a prepayment penalty on your mortgage, you can do this yourself at no cost.)

Houses and mortgages are another area where you need to dig deep, and ask yourself what you really want. Owning a big house is the American Dream. Is it your dream? When you really think about the things that are important to you, do you want a big house that will require you to work at a job an extra 10 years, or do you want a little house that will give you more flexibility? Do you want the responsibility of a house at all, or are you one of those people who would prefer to rent and have other people do the worrying?

Think about these things, and any barriers that might come up, due to scripting and beliefs, that might be blocking you from keeping your home situation consistent with your values. If you want to make a change, think about where you are in the change process, and apply the right techniques.

Bankruptcy

If you are thinking about bankruptcy, we would recommend you go to a credit counseling service first. If they really feel that there is no other choice, they will help you with the process.

But think twice or three times about bankruptcy before you do it. In fact, Stacey and I think there is only one reason to go through the process: when you have had a catastrophic event occur that you do not foresee happening again. A major medical disaster can strike anyone, and if you are uninsured or underinsured, you may simply acquire a debt burden that you cannot pay off.

There are four different types of bankruptcy protection. Chapter 7 is usually the option for people with a lot of credit card debt. Chapter 7 filings wipe away all of your debts. Chapter 13 filings require you to repay some funds over a period of several years. They are used in limited circumstances, such as protecting a home from foreclosure. Chapter 11 filings are used primarily for businesses wanting to reorganize. Finally, chapter 12 filings are specifically for farmers.

Recent changes in the laws have made filing more restrictive. In addition, bankruptcy will leave a big black mark on your credit report for 7 to 10 years.

If you decide to move forward, you'll want an attorney to walk you through the process. Check out the National Association of Consumer

Bankruptcy Attorneys for a lawyer in your area. They can be contacted at www.nacba.com.

Your Bottom Line

Let's move forward with your financial planning, but first make sure you've noted your debt and any of the dollar adjustments you plan to make to pay for it into your Bottom Line.

CHAPTER

13

Living Longer and Stronger

THE NEW RETIREMENT

We are living longer, stronger lives than ever before. At 60, many Baby Boomers are starting businesses and pursuing their passions. They are making plans to see the world. They are doing work to make it a better place. At 40, Generation X feels like they've just hit their stride. Many are just starting families. Talk to people in their 20s and 30s and those old models of moving up the corporate ladder as quickly as possible are simply gone. Their generation doesn't feel those kinds of pressures.

While we are all grateful for our longer lives, it also means that there is more to plan and pay for. This is challenging on many levels:

- We're facing the highest health care bills in history for ourselves and our parents.
- Families are using assets meant to be inherited by their children to pay for things like retirement and nursing homes.
- Social Security may be at risk.
- Corporate retirement benefits are changing their structure from the old defined benefit (pension) model to the newer defined contribution (401(k), 403(b)) model.

All of this comes at a time when we have the highest debt levels and the lowest savings on record. One of the many reasons Stacey and I think Life Planning is so important to current generations is that we simply cannot afford to blindly allocate time and money to assets and ideals that aren't part of our core values.

Your Ideal Retirement

Let's make sure that your financial resources are working to create the retirement of your dreams. We'll start by figuring out what your ideal retirement looks like. This may, of course, change over time, but you can always come back to this process and make the necessary adjustments.

Think about the following questions, and take some notes:

- What five things do you absolutely want to do in retirement?
- Who among your older friends, family, or role models has the kind of life you would like to have? What do you like about it? What steps do you think you can take to bring those things into your own retirement plans?
- Do you want to work when you retire? Would you like to do something other than what you are doing now? What will your finances have to look like to support that goal? For example, you may be downsizing and will need fewer resources. You may want to start a business, so you need to save more, and so on.
- Do you want to travel when you retire? How often? Where are the places you would like to go?
- How many "creature comforts" do you think you'll need in retirement? Do you absolutely need a big house? Is an expensive car important to you? What is a necessity and what is excess?
- What kind of community do you want to be a part of?
- Where is that community located?

_____

_____

_____

_____

_____

Now we need to figure out what your ideal retirement costs. Let's start by constructing your "dream week" for this time of your life. Here's a sample to get you started.

An Ideal Week in Retirement

	Morning	Afternoon	Evening
Sunday	Church	Long walk	Book club
Monday	Gym	Spanish course	Homework
Tuesday	Errands	Lawn care	Letters and e-mails to friends
Wednesday	Groceries	Volunteer work	Dinner and movie
Thursday	Gym	Spanish course	Homework
Friday	Clean house	Long walk	Letters and e-mails to friends
Saturday	Garden	Volunteer work	Dinner with friends

Now construct your own:

Your Ideal Week in Retirement

	Morning	Afternoon	Evening
Sunday			
Monday			
Tuesday			
Wednesday			
Thursday			
Friday			
Saturday			

Now that you know what your ideal retirement looks like, you'll need to know how much it's going to cost you. Look at the ideal week you charted above. Expand on it so that it's a month. Now think about the monthly expenses you identified in your Bottom Line. We're going to use them as a guide to estimate your monthly expenses when you retire. Some of these numbers will change when you retire. For example, if you aren't working, you won't need disability insurance. You won't be commuting to work. You won't need work clothes. You may eat out less now that you have time to cook. You'll probably travel more, at least in the first few years. Medical costs, particularly for prescription drugs, may rise. If you see obvious places on the expense chart where you can make some estimates, go ahead and do so. If not, don't worry; this gives us a general idea of what your monthly expenses will look like.

Monthly expenses:
Allowances
Charity
Child care
Clothing
Education
Food
Gifts
Hobbies
Housing
Maintenance
Medical
Miscellaneous
Self-care
Taxes
Transportation
Travel
Utilities

Insurance:
Health
Long-term care
Disability
Home
Auto
Other

Total monthly expenses:

The Cost of Inflation

You already know that $50,000 today will not be $50,000 tomorrow. You must consider the impact of inflation. Table 13.1 inflates annual expenses over different time periods.

Table 13.2 shows the lump sum of money you'll need when you retire to pay for your annual expenses. It assumes a 4 percent withdrawal rate. That's financial planner-speak for: You can take 4 percent of the lump sum out in your first year of retirement. You will be able to adjust that number for inflation each of the following years. Most planners work with a withdrawal rate somewhere around 4 percent. The number comes from extensive research done by financial planner Bill Bengen in the 1990s and by many others since then.

Here's how the chart works: Let's say you've figured out that you need $50,000 per year in retirement. You plan to retire in 20 years.

Table 13.1   **Future Expenses**

Annual Expenses	What Your Expenses Would Be In ...				
	5	10	20	30	40 Years at 3% Inflation
$20,000	$23,185	$26,878	$36,122	$48,545	$65,241
50,000	57,964	67,196	90,306	121,363	163,102
75,000	86,946	100,794	135,458	182,045	244,653
100,000	115,927	134,392	180,611	242,726	326,204
200,000	231,855	268,783	361,222	485,452	652,408

Table 13.2   **The Lump Sum You Would Need at Retirement to Generate an Annual Income for 30 Years If You Retire This Many Years from Now ...**

	5	10	20	30	40
$20,000	$579,637	$671,958	$903,056	$1,213,631	$1,631,019
50,000	1,449,093	1,679,958	2,257,639	3,034,078	4,077,547
75,000	2,173,639	2,519,843	3,386,459	4,551,117	6,116,321
100,000	2,898,185	3,359,791	4,515,278	6,068,156	8,155,094
200,000	5,796,370	6,719,582	9,030,556	12,136,312	16,310,189

Table 13.3   **How Much You Would Need to Save Each Month at a 7% Tax-Deferred Return to Get to the Income Amount You Need**

	5	10	20	30	40
$20,000	$8,049	$3,860	$1,724	$989	$618
50,000	20,123	9,649	4,309	2,473	1,544
75,000	30,185	14,474	6,463	3,709	2,317
100,000	40,247	19,299	8,618	4,945	3,089
200,000	80,493	38,597	17,235	9,890	6,178

At 3 percent inflation, you will need $90,306 in 20 years to buy what $50,000 buys now. You will need a lump sum of $2,257,639 to generate that $90,306 in the first year alone! See Table 13.2.

As you can see, the numbers are big when it comes to retirement planning! Before we figure out how to adjust your finances so that you can meet your retirement goals, let's take into consideration money that you have already saved and Social Security (see Table 13.4).

In spite of all the dire warnings about Social Security, most experts believe that it will still be around in some form, though it may be taxed more in the future. To factor in your Social Security amounts, there are calculators available at www.ssa.gov.

Table 13.4   If You Have Current Savings, This Is What They Will Be Worth Tomorrow . . .

Current Savings	5	10	20	30	40 Years at 7% Return
$20,000	$28,051	$39,343	$77,394	$152,245	$299,489
50,000	70,128	98,358	193,484	380,613	748,723
75,000	105,191	147,536	290,226	570,919	1,123,084
100,000	140,255	196,715	386,968	761,226	1,497,446
200,000	280,510	393,430	773,937	1,522,451	2,994,892
500,000	701,276	983,576	1,934,842	3,806,128	7,487,229
1,000,000	1,402,552	1,967,151	3,869,684	7,612,255	14,974,458

The calculator will either give you benefit amounts in current dollars or future dollars. Use current dollars. Here's an example: Let's say your income needs in retirement are $75,000. The Social Security calculator says that you will get $25,000 in current dollars. That means you will need to generate $50,000 from other sources. If you are retiring in 20 years, that amount is $2,257,639. If you already have $100,000 saved, you can subtract $386,968 from that sum, leaving you $1,870,671 left to accumulate in the next 20 years. That's 83 percent of $2,257,639. So you need to save 83 percent of $4,309, or $3,644 per month. Determine how your current retirement savings affect your savings targets. Put the additional amount you should be saving in order to reach your goals into your Bottom Line.

If these calculations make your eyeballs glaze over, or if you want to really hone in on the numbers rather than use than the approximations shown here, there are any number of calculators out on the Web. We have heard good reports about T. Rowe Price's, but just type "retirement calculator" into any search engine.

The Messages You've Received about Retirement

Many of us had important people in our lives when we were growing up that were in their "Golden Years." The way we saw them behave was creating our own expectations about this time of life whether we realized it or not. In addition, the ways in which your parents or primary caregivers prepared for this part of their life also impacted your perceptions. Maybe they didn't think or talk about it at all. It's important that we identify how these impressions are playing out in your behavior today.

Take a look at "How the Financial Lessons We Learned from Our Parents Affect the Choices We Make as Adults" at the end of Chapter 4. Do you see any ways in which the lessons you learned when you were young are playing out in your retirement planning? What do you think of those lessons now? What are the thoughts and behaviors you'll adapt to transcend those early messages if they don't serve you? How can you build on them if they are consistent with your values? Take some notes if it will help you gain clarity on this issue. Also, put FS (family scripts) in the designated space in your Bottom Line if these early lessons are not serving your best interests.

_____

_____

_____

_____

_____

Even though we're living longer, healthier lives, societal pressures lead many of us to live beyond our means. Retirement planning often gets pushed off. I know of many people who have tapped into their 401(k)s to fund their current lifestyle. Look at "Your Story" at the end of Chapter 5, to see if you identified social pressures like "keeping up with the Joneses." Messages about gender, race, and ethnicity can also impact your savings and expectations for this time of life. Take some notes if it helps you clarify these influences. Also, put SS in the space designated for scripts in the retirement row of your Bottom Line if these scripts are working against your higher goals.

_____

_____

_____

_____

_____

What about those little voices that sing in our heads? What tunes do they sing when you think about planning for retirement: "I'm not going to worry about it," "I'm right on track"? Are these messages playing out in your financial behavior? Jot them down, and think of some songs and behaviors that will drown out those old tunes! If the messages you tell yourself about retirement planning play out in your financial behavior, put IS (internal script), in the "Scripts" column in the "Savings" row of your Bottom Line.

_____

_____

_____

_____

_____

If you've decided to make some changes to the financial side of your retirement planning, where do you think you are in the change process? Again, here are the six stages Dr. Prochaska and his colleagues identified and the abbreviations you should use on your Bottom Line as you put that information onto the chart.

1. Precontemplation (PC)
2. Contemplation (C)
3. Preparation (P)
4. Action (A)
5. Maintenance (M)
6. Termination (T)

Review the techniques that will allow you to move out of that stage. Also, look at the notes you took on how to make each of the techniques work for you. You may want to jot some of those down, so that you can refer to them during this chapter. In addition, use the following abbreviations to note those change techniques in the "Technique" column on your Bottom Line.

- Consciousness raising (CR)
- Social liberation (SL)
- Emotional arousal (EA)
- Self-reevaluation (SR)
- Commitment (C)
- Countering (CT)
- Environment control (EC)
- Reward (R)
- Helping relationships (HR)

_____

_____

_____

Achieving Your Goals

If it all sounds like too much, don't despair. You have lots of options. You can:

- Save hard starting right now.
- Work a little bit longer. Working one or two more years can make a tremendous difference in both the amount of money you can save and the amount of money you will need.
- Reallocate your assets—sell a second home or car, for example, and apply that money toward your goals.
- Work part-time in retirement.
- Move someplace that's less expensive to live.
- Make sure your investments are properly allocated for your time horizon and risk tolerance (we'll talk more about that in another chapter).

When it comes to saving and investing for retirement, put away the amount you need to save each month before you start spending. This will greatly increase your chances of achieving your savings targets.

And make sure you record those amounts in your Bottom Line.

Where to Save for Retirement

The best place to put your money, hands down, is in a 401(k), 403(b), or 457 plan at work. Those strange numbers just refer to sections of the Internal Revenue Code. The plans are similar in most ways—which one you have will depend on whether you work for a company, a not-for-profit organization, or a governmental entity.

Why put your money there? Two big reasons: (1) the money you put in these plans is tax-deferred until you take it out, and (2) it's easy to save—all you have to do is enroll and pick some investments. Money will be taken out of your paycheck automatically. In fact, in some places, you are automatically enrolled once you start work.

If you contribute money to a tax-deferred plan, something interesting happens. Your taxes go down. Let's say you are in the 25 percent federal marginal tax bracket. In that case, every dollar you put into your plan costs you only 75 cents. That's because that money is not taxed in that year. It's as if you never earned the money.

Your company may also have a matching contribution. Say they contribute 50 cents for every dollar you put in, up to 5 percent of your pay. If you make $50,000 per year, and you put in $2,500, or 5 percent of your pay, the company will put in $1,250. So at the end of the year you will show contributions to the plan of $3,750. But with the tax advantage, it will have only cost you $1,875. That's an immediate return on your investment of 50 percent!

What is even better is the way the money will grow, tax-deferred, over time. That $3,750 annual contribution will grow to $163,441 after 20 years (assume biweekly contributions and a 7 percent return). Put in the current maximum, $15,500, and, using the same assumptions, it will grow to $676,463.

Many people don't contribute to their retirement plans at work because they don't know where to put their money. Companies are starting to introduce "target date retirement funds" into their plans. They are a great option if investments are the *last* thing you ever want to think about.

These funds have all kinds of investments in them, so you get a diversified portfolio with just one fund. The target date is in the name of the fund, for example, "Target Date 2020 Fund." All you have to do is pick the one closest to your age 65 (or the date you plan to retire), and the fund will do the rest. Your money can even stay in the fund after you retire, since all of these funds become income-oriented 5 to 10 years after the target retirement date.

Roth 401(k)

Roth 401(k) and 403(b) plans are just starting to find their way into company pension plans. People can elect to contribute pre-tax to a regular 401(k) or after-tax to a Roth. With a Roth, the money goes in after tax, but it is tax-free coming out. That can make great sense for people in their 20s and 30s, who can build up a lot of money over time and not pay taxes on it. Roths also make sense for high earners who expect to pay just as much in taxes after they retire as they do now.

Retirement Plans When You Are Self-Employed, Have Income from a Second Job, or Do Not Have a Plan at Work

You have several options:

Simplified Employee Pensions.   Simplified employee pensions (SEPs) allow you to contribute (and also deduct) up 20 percent of your self-employment income. That number rises to 25 percent of salary if you have your own company. You can vary the amount each year. The maximum dollar contribution is $45,000. You must make your contribution by the time your tax return is due, and you can establish the plan at the same time. The paperwork is minimal.

Keoghs.   Keogh plans are like company retirement programs for the self-employed. There are both profit-sharing and pension Keoghs. The plan must be established before the end of the year in which you want to make the contribution, but the contribution itself does not need to be made by the due date for your tax return. Keoghs require more paperwork than SEPs. You need the plan document and an annual report.

Profit-sharing Keoghs have contribution limits similar to the SEP—you can contribute 20 percent of self-employment income or 25 percent if you are compensated as an employee. Also like the SEP, the maximum dollar contribution is $45,000 for 2007.

Defined-benefit Keoghs are designed to deliver an annual retirement benefit, which can be as high as $180,000. To determine your contribution, an actuary must be involved, since there are many variables in the calculation. The actuarial fees tend to make this the most expensive type of plan, but it may also allow the largest contribution.

Solo 401(k)s.   Solo 401(k)s let you contribute up to 100 percent of the first $15,500 of your compensation or self-employment income for the tax year 2007. That amount rises to $20,500 if you are at least 50 or turn 50 by year-end. You can contribute additionally up to 25 percent of your compensation income or 20 percent of your self-employment income. The plan needs to be established by the end of the applicable year.

If You Are an Employer.   If you have a plan, generally your employees must be covered as well. You should talk to your accountant, pension consultant, or attorney before proceeding further.

Roth IRAs.   These are different from the Roth 401(k) mentioned in the last section. The money still goes in after taxes, but they have much lower limits. For 2007, you can make contributions up to $4,000 for singles and $8,000 for couples. There are income limits. Your ability to make a contribution to a Roth IRA starts to phase out when your adjusted gross income reaches $99,000 and phases out completely at $114,000 for singles ($156,000 and $166,000 for joint filers). You can still have a company 401(k), 403(b), or any of the plans listed above when you have a Roth IRA. You can also contribute an additional $1,000 if you will be 50 or older at year-end.

Other Things to Consider in Your Retirement Planning

One thing my husband and I know for certain—we won't be retiring in New Jersey. We own a little postwar split level. Its size and location are perfect for us. Because of its location, however, it cost a lot of money. Add to that the fact that our real estate taxes are through the roof. While we're both working, we can afford high real estate taxes, but afterwards, when we're on a fixed income? That's money we would much rather spend elsewhere. So, even though we're about a decade away from a permanent change, we've started to explore other, more affordable areas of this and other countries. Joe speaks Spanish and I've always wanted to learn, so Spain or Mexico or Central or South America might be possibilities.

If housing prices and real estate taxes are a concern, stay away from California and the New York area. Explore towns and cities inland. I recently spoke with a couple who moved from Brooklyn to a small town in the mountains of North Carolina. They love the climate, the golf, and the friendliness of their neighbors.

Wherever you decide to live in retirement, try it out first. Take a few vacations there. Think about renting for a year or two before you buy. Yes, maybe your best friends just moved there. But are you in 100 percent agreement with everything your best friends think?

Using Real Estate to Fund Your Retirement

When people from areas with stratospheric real estate prices talk to me about retirement planning, the subject of home equity always comes up. They figure they can use their real estate to fund all or most of their retirement. It's a logical thought in Manhattan, where the average co-op now costs more than $1 million. And no, I did not make that number up!

If the retirement home of their dreams is in Guttenberg, Iowa (a beautiful place, by the way—right on the banks of the Mississippi and straight out of a picture postcard), they might be right. If not, they need to give serious thought to where they want to live and how far their real estate assets will get them.

Many people think they will save money by downscaling their home. That's not necessarily true. Home builders see a trend for small but luxuriously appointed homes for retirees. It may have less square footage, but it also may have a Viking range, a Jacuzzi, and a golf course abutting the backyard.

For that reason, many financial planners don't count home equity as a retirement asset. People who have expensive houses while they are working tend to have expensive houses when they retire.

Reverse Mortgages.   While we're on the topic of housing, we should talk about reverse mortgages. (Reverse mortgages provide a series of payments, based on the value of the house, in exchange for all or part of the equity from the sale of the house.) There are a lot of people out there who plan to rely on a reverse mortgage when they run out of money. Is this a good idea? Not usually. Before you plan on it, there are a few things you need to understand. A reverse mortgage ties you to your house. As long as you live in your house, the reverse mortgage does not come due. The minute you sell it, however, you owe the money. Then what are you going to do?

If you know that you are going to stay in a house until you die, then the reverse mortgage approach works. But circumstances change—that's why I suggest reverse mortgages as a last resort, not a primary retirement planning tool.

Wellness

The Baby Boomers may be the first generation who will spend more years in retirement than they did working. We are living a long time nowadays—just ask Willard Scott.

I once did financial planning for a couple in their 50s. All four parents were alive and well and they had four living grandparents. If there is such a thing as a longevity gene, these people had it. It made their retirement planning mighty complicated—what age should I assume they would live to? Would age 100 be long enough? They were amused until they realized what it meant—they might have to fund more than 35 years of retirement past age 65.

What good is a long life without health? Here are some questions to ask yourself in preparing to live the rest of your life as healthfully as you can:

- Do you make time for yourself?
- Do you get enough sleep?
- Do you have a healthy way of dealing with stress?
- Do you incorporate movement into your life?
- Are you eating healthfully?
- Do you make time for friends and family?
- Do you make time for laughter?
- Have you found a work/life balance that works?

It's important to think about how you will keep yourself healthy in retirement, and if it costs money, it should be included in your financial planning.

The Sandwich Generation

Living longer, stronger lives means that just as you are experiencing freedom as your children grow, your parents may need you more. And your children may rely on you for financial assistance long after they might have been expected to have left the nest. What's a sandwich to do?

Love Your Parents.   One of my wisest friends was sitting with her parents and in-laws at Thanksgiving dinner. Her mother asked her what she wanted for Christmas. Annette took a deep breath, and announced to the room that all she wanted from her elders was a letter from each of them stating their wishes if something happened and some guidance as to where their important documents were kept. Because she had the courage to ask, she got those letters and had the most stress-free Christmas in years.

Love is about communication. Make sure you understand your parents' wants and needs while they are able to express them. Give your parents a copy of this book and have them go through the exercises so that they can clarify those wants and needs for themselves.

Once you have done that work, have a conversation about money, alone if you can, or with an impartial third party if you cannot.

You need to understand if your parents will require your financial support. If they will, the further ahead you know, the more you can prepare yourself. If you have siblings, they need to be a part of the conversation, too.

Love Your Children.   Loving your children is not just about financial support. Love is also about independence. As a financial planner, I see many parents risk their retirement by dipping into their retirement savings for their adult children. Resist the temptation. The financial burden on your children could increase if you can't support your lifestyle after you retire.

There are kids who can't take care of themselves. And by that I do not mean the ones born without a psychic backbone, but those who have physical and/or mental conditions that keep them from fully participating in the working world. For them, find a good trusts and estates planner who specializes in special-needs kids, and work out a plan. There are very effective trusts that can be set up to help them.

Love is also about communication. Make sure you understand your children's goals so that you can help them make the move to independence. Give your children a copy of this book and have them go through the exercises so that they can clarify those wants and needs for themselves.

Your Bottom Line

What do you want your retirement to look like? How much money do you need to save to make it happen? You've had a lot to consider. Make sure your monthly savings needs for retirement are accurately reflected in your Bottom Line.

CHAPTER 14

Covering Your Assets

HOW TO CHOOSE THE RIGHT INSURANCE

You've worked hard to channel your resources toward your most important goals. Life is rolling along happily, and you're spending your time and money on the things that matter most to you. Then the unexpected happens. Aunt Betty comes over for dinner and slips and falls on your stairs. Uncle Chuck sees this as the big payday he's been waiting for, and you don't have a lot of liability insurance. Next thing you know, your time, and some of the money you have earmarked for your goals, is going toward your aunt's medical bills and lawyer fees.

On the flip side, I've come across many people who are so concerned about having insurance for a rainy day that they pay for policies they simply don't need. I know a couple in their 50s, for example, who did not have children or grandchildren, but were spending a lot on life insurance. (There are a lot of scripts out there that tell us that life insurance is a must.) After reevaluating how this scripting was playing out in their financial choices, they took the money they were spending on insurance and used it to supplement their investments for retirement.

Having the right insurance will protect from the financial devastation that can come with the unexpected. You want to make sure you are protecting the things that are most important to you, but in an efficient manner. We will walk you through the essentials so that you have the information you need to make the right choices.

First, let's break down insurance into two categories:

1. Insurance you should have
2. Insurance that depends on your situation and priorities

Insurance You Should Have

- You should have **health insurance**. According to a study by *Health Affairs Journal*, half of all personal bankruptcies are due to health care costs.
- **Dental insurance** falls into the same category. We mention it separately, because it normally is a separate policy.
- **Long-term care insurance** is necessary if you are over 50 and not poor or a multimillionaire. (Some planners would like you to have it even earlier.) If you have very few assets, you may not need long-term care insurance, because Medicaid may cover you.
- **Long-term disability insurance** is necessary if (1) you are working, (2) it is not provided by your employer, and (3) you or your family depend on your income. You normally do not need it once you have retired.
- **Homeowner's insurance** is important if you own a home or rent an apartment and want to protect the contents. If you have a mortgage, your mortgage bank will require it. It is also important because it offers you liability protection in case of a lawsuit.
- **Auto insurance** is required by your state if you drive a car. It offers you liability protection as well.

Insurance that Depends on Your Situation and Priorities

- In the event of your death, **life insurance** helps protect people who are dependent on your income. Once you have accumulated sufficient assets (typically by retirement), it may no longer be needed.
- **Short-term disability insurance** may be important for you to have if it is not provided by your state or your employer and you do not have enough money set aside to cover 6 to 12 months of living expenses until long-term disability kicks in.

- **Accidental death and dismemberment insurance** is meant to insure you in the unlikely event that you die or are maimed in an accident. You need to think about your priorities and your dependents as you decide if you need this inexpensive insurance.
- **Umbrella liability coverage** is important to consider if you have considerable assets, generally $1 million or more.
- **Insurance riders** on your homeowner's policy are for special items that you would want to replace. You may not want it, for example, for a one-of-a-kind family heirloom that you would never replace anyway.

As we get a clearer picture on the insurance you need to protect the things that are most important to you, let's see if there are any scripts at work in this aspect of your financial planning.

Money Scripts and Insurance

I actually want to start by having you look at the societal messages that may be working on your insurance choices. This is a big thing for men. As Stacey discussed in Part I, men see their ability to provide and protect as a big part of their identity. This leads some to carry insurance they don't need. We call that *overprotecting*. Overprotection is an understandable urge, but it actually becomes a liability when it costs money you could be using somewhere else. Do you see any societal scripts in your choices about insurance? Maybe it's not over-protection, but a belief that you don't know enough about money to make these complex choices? A social message to be a risk taker? Messages to "keep up" that force you to neglect this part of your finances, because you're using the money for something else? Take a look at "Your Story" in Chapter 5. Is there anything you identified that may be at work in your choices about insurance? Take some notes. If you see a tendency that you should keep in mind when you allocate money to this part of your finances, put SS (societal script) in the designated column of your Bottom Line.

_____

_____

_____

_____

_____

Are any of the lessons you learned when you were growing up affecting your choices about insurance? Did your parents or primary caregivers have concerns about scarcity that made them overprotective? Did they have a "devil may care" attitude in some of their financial behavior that may have sent a message that insurance is unimportant? Did they give you enough information about their financial beliefs for you to formulate an opinion about insurance, or were you left to come up with your own ideas. Look at "Your Story" at the end of Chapter 4 and the notes you took earlier in the chapter about your parents' or primary caregivers' lessons and attitudes about money. If you see anything that may be playing out in your decisions about protecting your priorities, put FS (family script) in the designated column of your Bottom Line.

_____

_____

_____

_____

_____

What thoughts come to mind when you think about life insurance, health insurance, insurance to cover your home, long-term care insurance, liability insurance, disability insurance, and so on? Are these messages consistent with your values? Do you see a disconnect in your core values and your behavior? Take at look at "Your Story" at the end of Chapter 6. Do you notice any "songs" that may be playing out in your choices about insurance? If you think there are any that could be drowning out your true beliefs and values, you'll want to note this on your Bottom Line. Put IS (internal script) in the designated column.

_____

_____

_____

_____

_____

If you want to make some changes to the financial side of your insurance planning, where do you think you are in the change process? Maybe you're contemplating this because you've never thought of insurance in this way. Again, here are the six stages Dr. Prochaska and his colleagues identified, and the abbreviations you should use on your Bottom Line as you put that information onto the chart.

1. Precontemplation (PC)
2. Contemplation (C)
3. Preparation (P)
4. Action (A)
5. Maintenance (M)
6. Termination (T)

Review the techniques that will allow you to move out of that stage. Also, look at the notes you took on how to make each of the techniques work for you. You may want to jot some of those down, so that you can refer to them during this chapter. In addition, use the following abbreviations to note those change techniques in the "Technique" column on your Bottom Line.

- Consciousness raising (CR)
- Social liberation (SL)
- Emotional arousal (EA)
- Self-reevaluation (SR)
- Commitment (C)
- Countering (CT)
- Environment control (EC)
- Reward (R)
- Helping relationships (HR)

_____

_____

_____

_____

_____

Now, let's decide the types of insurance that will work best for you.

The Right Insurance for You

Health Insurance

The first insurance you need to think about is health insurance. Unless you are extremely wealthy or are immune to illness, this is your first line of defense. You can buy your own health insurance policy, but normally, the least expensive way for you to obtain health insurance is through your job.

There are a number of different kinds of health insurance. They have a variety of names and fall into the following broad categories:

- *High-deductible policies* combine with a health savings account (HSA). These provide coverage after you have paid a large deductible. You can pay for the deductible amounts from your HSA. Unlike flexible spending accounts, you can carry the HSA money over from year to year. If you are healthy and do not incur many medical expenses, the HSA can become another form of savings. The premiums for this kind of insurance tend to be low, but your out-of-pocket costs can be high. Recent changes in the tax law have made these policies worth looking into.
- *Traditional indemnity policies* are the oldest kind of health insurance. The premiums are high, but participants are free to make their own decisions about health care. Because of cost, however, these plans are relatively rare.
- *Health maintenance organizations* (HMOs) have no deductible and no copays, but restrict your access to their network of hospitals and physicians. You have a primary physician who serves as a gatekeeper to your health services. Go outside, and you're on your own.
- *Preferred provider organizations* (PPOs) have two tiers of service: You can use in-network for lower costs, or out-of-network for higher costs.
- *Point of service plans* (POSs) have gatekeeper physicians, like HMOs, but like PPOs, allow you to go out of the network if you pay a higher percentage of the cost.

Comparing Health Insurance Policies.   Many employers offer more than one type of insurance. How do you know which to choose? Use your own experience. Take a look at your medical expenses for last year and see how the plans offered would cover them. Look at three factors:

1. Insurance premiums—the amount that comes out of your paycheck.
2. Deductibles—the amount you need to pay before your insurance kicks in.
3. Copays—the amount you pay once your deductible is covered.

Dental Insurance

This is usually available at low cost through your employer. It covers an annual exam and cleaning, but has large copays for work that is necessary but expensive, like crowns.

Since preventive dental care is an important part of your overall health, and since you are much more likely to get the care you need if you have insurance, we want you to have this.

Retiree Health Insurance

Options if you are under age 65 include:

- Getting coverage on your spouse's policy if he or she is still working.
- Retiree medical if your company offers it.
- COBRA (Consolidated Omnibus Budget Reconciliation Act of 1985) for 18 months after retiring (36 months under special circumstances.) You will pay the entire cost of your medical policy, but at the company's rate. There is an additional 2 percent administrative surcharge.
- Individual policies—normally, the highest cost.

If you are age 65 or older, your default will normally be Medicare, unless you are still working. There's a pretty good Web site (www. medicare.gov) where you will find a publication called *Medicare and You*. It covers many of the details. But here it is in short:

- Medicare Part A—Hospital. For most people, this is automatic, and does not have to be paid for. You paid the premiums while you were working. If you never paid Medicare premiums, you may have to pay for this.

- Medicare Part B—Medical. For most people, this goes along with Part A, but there is an additional premium you must pay.
- Medigap. This covers the "gaps" in Part A and B coverage, such as dental care, lab tests, eye care, routine physicals, shots, diabetic supplies, hearing aids, and some deductibles. Medigap is sold by private insurance companies.
- Medicare Part C—Medicare Advantage Plans. These plans normally cover the same services as Parts A and B, and Medigap, and may also provide prescription drug coverage and other additional services. There are widely varying costs. Here are the main types:
  - Preferred Provider Organization Plan
  - Health Maintenance Organization Plan
  - Fee-for-Service Plan
  - Special-Needs Plan, for those with certain chronic illnesses and other specialized health needs
  - Medical Savings Account Plan—combines a high-deductible health care plan with a savings account
- Medicare Part D—Prescription Drug Coverage.

Note: Long-term care is *not* covered under any of these plans.

Disability Insurance

Studies show that a 20-year-old worker has a 3-in-10 chance of becoming disabled before reaching retirement age (*Source:* www.ssa.gov). You need disability insurance if you are dependent on income and don't live off of your savings or investments.

Disability insurance provides benefits if you are ill or injured. It is normally based on a percentage of your income. There are two main types: short term and long term.

Short-Term Disability.   Short-term disability insurance covers you if you are disabled for a short period of time, typically 180 days or less, but sometimes up to a year.

"Five states (New York, New Jersey, Rhode Island, California, and Hawaii) and Puerto Rico mandate that employers provide some short-term disability coverage, or provide it through a state-funded program" (*Wall Street Journal,* December 19, 2006). For others, insurance may be available on the job or through a private policy.

Do you need short-term disability insurance? Yes, unless you have enough money set aside to cover 6 to 12 months of expenses, or your family does not need your income. Normally, the policy covers a set percentage of income. Your employer may pay for a certain percentage, and then you can "buy up" to another percentage.

The strangest thing about disability insurance is that in almost every case *except disability insurance,* it's better to pay for things pretax. Because of a twist in the tax law, if you pay for disability insurance pretax, your benefits are taxable. If you pay after tax, your benefits are tax free.

You may not have a choice about this. If your employer pays for your insurance, your benefits will normally be taxable. But if you have a choice, pay for your insurance after tax.

Long-Term Disability.   Long-term disability policies begin, logically enough, where short-term disability policies leave off.

One type of long-term disability insurance is available through the federal government. It's called Social Security disability.

Social Security Disability (www.ssa.gov/disability/).   Social Security disability is based on your inability to work. Social Security considers you disabled if you cannot do work that you did before and Social Security determines that you cannot adjust to other work because of your medical condition(s). Your disability must also last or be expected to last for at least one year or to result in death. In order to qualify, you must be employed in a job covered by Social Security.

Social Security disability is notoriously difficult to qualify for. Most people would consider themselves to be disabled long before they passed Social Security's stringent tests.

Other Forms of Disability Compensation.   In addition to Social Security disability, there are other forms of compensation that may be available to you if you are disabled:

- Workers' compensation for work-related injuries or illnesses, required in all states.
- Special disability programs for veterans injured in war, federal and state government workers, railroad employees, or miners who develop black lung disease.

- State vocational rehabilitation programs.
- Automobile insurance benefits for a disability resulting from an auto accident.

Source: Federal Citizen Information Center.

But just about everyone reading this book should make sure they have their own long-term disability coverage, either through their employer or as an individual policy. Your employer may offer group coverage that could be much cheaper than an individual product. That's the first place you should look. But get a quote for at least one individual policy as well. Costs can vary widely.

What's the right amount for you? Think of how much money you need to live on. You've already done the work for that in the previous chapters. Following is a checklist that will help you on your search:

Disability Policy Checklist (from the Association of Health Insurance Advisors)*

Things you should know before buying a disability policy:

1. How is disability defined?
   - Inability to perform your own job?
   - Inability to perform any job?
2. Does the policy cover:
   - Accidents?
   - Illness?
3. Are benefits available:
   - For total disability?
   - For partial disability?
   - Only after total disability?
4. Are full benefits paid, whether or not you are able to work for loss of:
   - Sight?
   - Speech?
   - Hearing?
   - Use of limbs?

---

*The Disability Policy Checklist is intended for information only; decisions should be based on individual circumstances. This checklist is not a substitute for advice from a licensed insurance professional or legal counsel.

5. The maximum benefit will replace what percentage of income?
6. Is the policy noncancelable, guaranteed renewable, or conditionally renewable?
7. How long must I be disabled before premiums are waived?
8. Is there an option to buy additional coverage, without evidence of insurability, at a later date?
9. Does the policy offer an inflation adjustment feature? If so:
   • What is the rate of inflation?
   • Is there a maximum?

Long-Term Care Insurance

Long-term care insurance protects you in the event that you are no longer able to care for yourself. Do you need it? Yes, unless (1) you have no dependents and don't mind exhausting your assets if you require care or (2) you can afford to pay for the cost of a nursing home out-of-pocket. In the New York City area, where Stacey and I live, that can run to $100,000 per year or more.

Many people feel that Medicare or other health insurance will take care of this need, but it generally does not. You may be eligible for long-term care through Medicaid, however, if you have very limited means.

Medicare pays for "medically necessary skilled nursing facility or home health care," but there are a large number of restrictions on who qualifies and under what circumstances. (*Source:* www.medicare.gov)

The term *activities of daily living* is key when it comes to long-term care, because your lack of ability to perform them will determine your eligibility, Here's what they are:

• Dressing
• Toileting
• Bathing
• Eating
• Continence
• Transferring (moving into or out of a bed, chair, or wheelchair)

Long-Term Care Policy Checklist.* Before you begin shopping, you should find out how much nursing home or home health care costs in your area today. If you needed care right away, could you find it locally or would you have to go to another, potentially more expensive area? Once you've done some research, you can use the following checklist to help you compare policies you may be considering.

1. What services are covered?
    *   Nursing home care
    *   Home health care
    *   Assisted living facility
    *   Adult daycare
    *   Alternate care
    *   Respite care
    *   Other
2. How much does the policy pay per day for nursing home care? For home health care? For an assisted living facility? For adult day care? For alternate care? For respite care? Other?
3. How long will benefits last in a nursing home? At home? In an assisted living facility? Other?
4. Does the policy have a maximum lifetime benefit? If so, what is it for nursing home care? For home health care? For an assisted living facility? Other?
5. Does the policy have a maximum length of coverage for each period of confinement? If so, what is it for nursing home care? For home health care? For an assisted living facility?
6. How long must I wait before preexisting conditions are covered?
7. How many days must I wait before benefits begin for nursing home care? For home health care? For an assisted living facility? Other?
8. Are Alzheimer's disease and other organic mental and nervous disorders covered?
9. Does this policy require an assessment of activities of daily living? An assessment of cognitive impairment? Physician certification of need? A prior hospital stay for nursing home care? Home health care? A prior nursing home stay for home health care coverage? Other?

---

*The Consumer Guide to Long-Term Care Insurance, published by America's Health Insurance Plans. This checklist is intended for information only; decisions should be based on individual circumstances. This checklist is not a substitute for advice from a licensed insurance professional or legal counsel.

10. Is the policy guaranteed renewable?
11. What is the age range for enrollment?
12. Is there a waiver-of-premium provision for nursing home care? For home health care?
13. How long must I be confined before premiums are waived?
14. Does the policy have a nonforfeiture benefit?
15. Does the policy offer an inflation adjustment feature? If so, what is the rate of increase? How often is it applied? For how long? Is there an additional cost?
16. What does the policy cost?
    - Per year?
      - With inflation feature
      - Without inflation feature
      - With nonforfeiture feature
      - Without nonforfeiture feature
    - Per month?
      - With inflation feature
      - Without inflation feature
      - With nonforfeiture feature
      - Without nonforfeiture feature
17. Is there a 30-day free look?

Life Insurance

Do you need life insurance? Well, it depends. If you have no dependents and don't care whether you leave an estate, you may not. If you have substantial assets and have no desire to make arrangements for estate taxes, you also may not need it.

Rules of thumb don't work with life insurance. You may have heard it said that you should insure yourself for seven or eight times your income. Well, maybe or maybe not. There are so many factors. Years ago, I met in the same week with two young families who wanted me to calculate their insurance needs. They had sent me their paperwork, and the families were strikingly similar. Each family had two wage earners and two preschool-aged children. Family incomes were almost identical. Both couples were in their early 30s. Same insurance needs, right?

Wrong. You see, one family lived in the same neighborhood they had grown up in. They were surrounded by extended family. Their children spent their days with aunts and uncles and grandparents while the parents worked. That family had only basic insurance needs. Enough to pay off the mortgage, supplement income for a few years, provide for a small college fund. The extended family would take care of everything else.

The second family had moved east from Colorado. They had no extended family to speak of. If one of the couple passed away, the other would have to pay for everything on one income, including massive amounts of child care, with no family to turn to. Their insurance needs were much greater.

In order to figure out your life insurance needs yourself, you will need to do a present value calculation of the difference between cash flow now and cash flow needs in the event of your death. That difference represents your insurance needs.

A calculator can make this a lot easier! Try the one at http://moneycentral.msn.com/investor/calcs/n_life/main.asp.

Types of Life Insurance.   Believe it or not, life insurance is simpler than it looks. There are only two main types:

1. Cash value
2. Term

Cash value has many flavors now, but its ancestor is the old permanent or whole-life insurance policy that your parents probably owned. You paid a certain amount each month, for many years, then the policy became "paid up," and you had insurance for the rest of your life. There are three main problems with cash insurance:

1. It's expensive.
2. Inflation erodes the value of the policy over time.
3. If you save your money, you should not need insurance for your entire life.

Having said this, sooner or later an insurance person is going to try to sell you one of the new flavors—variable life, universal life, variable universal, or something that was invented last week and I haven't heard of yet. These policies have investment components, and there will be charts showing how much money you will have in 30 years if some really unusual things happen in the stock market. I can't promise you that these dreams won't come true. But I can tell you that most financial planners and chief financial officers I know buy term insurance and manage their investments separately.

For most people, the right insurance is term. Life insurance is basically designed to get the house paid off and the kids taken care of through college. Even if you buy it when your kids are born, you probably won't need it for more than 30 years. Term policies are inexpensive and becoming more so.

Is it possible you might need cash value insurance? Yes, if you have a need that will never go away. People who have dependents with disabilities may put cash value insurance into a trust for them. And cash value insurance can be used in an estate-planning tool called an irrevocable life insurance trust (ILIT). But these tools should not be used lightly. If you have a large estate or other complicated planning needs, then you need a financial planner and a trusts and estates attorney who like each other and will work with you to construct an estate plan.

Be sure to compare policies. If you have never heard of an insurance company, you can use one of the insurance ratings services mentioned later in the chapter to determine their financial strength.

Term Life Insurance Web Sites. There are many, but here are two that I use most often:

- www.selectquote.com
- www.realiaquote.com

Accidental Death and Dismemberment Insurance

Accidental death and dismemberment insurance is very inexpensive. That's because you are unlikely to die in an accident or become dismembered unless you work in a dangerous occupation. You should never regard this as a replacement for life insurance.

Property and Casualty Insurance

Property and casualty insurance protects your home, car, truck, boat, RV, and all other things of that type.

Auto insurance is required in all 50 states. What you must carry on your policy, however, varies. Generally, auto insurance has the following components:

- Liability
- Uninsured motorists coverage
- Personal injury protection
- Collision
- Comprehensive
- Other

Within the requirements for your state, you can choose the amount of your coverage and your deductible. The higher your coverage, the more you pay. The higher your deductible, the less you pay. Generally, planners recommend as high a deductible as you can afford.

Homeowner's insurance is not required everywhere, but if you have a mortgage, your lender will insist that you have it. And you should have it, whether you own or are renting. You will want to make sure that your coverage is for replacement cost, since the cost of rebuilding has gone up so much over time. A few other things to consider:

- Like auto insurance, the higher your deductible, the lower your premium. Choose the highest deductible you can afford.
- If you have expensive jewelry, antiques, or equipment, you will want to cover them with special riders. You may need an appraisal to do this.
- Flood insurance is not covered by your homeowner's policy. For that you need a policy through the federal government. Here's the Web site: www.floodsmart.gov.
- Read your policy carefully to see what other things are excluded.

If you have significant assets, consider putting umbrella liability coverage on top of your auto and homeowner's or renter's policies. It works just like it sounds—it provides an umbrella of protection on top of the coverage you already have. If your auto insurance and homeowner's insurance cover you for $500,000, for example, your umbrella coverage can take you to $1 million or more. It's generally inexpensive, and in our litigious society, useful.

This has been a lot of information, but we wanted to make sure you had the tools you need to make the choices that will protect what's important to you, in the most efficient way possible. Before we get to your Bottom Line cost for insurance, think about the following ways in which the company you choose can affect your costs.

General Information on Insurance Companies

How financially sound is your insurance company? There are ratings services to help you determine this. The Web sites of the four best-known—A. M. Best, Fitch, Moody's, and Standard & Poor's—are listed below. If your company has a low rating, then you might consider choosing an alternative.

- A. M. Best: www.ambest.com
- Fitch: www.fitchratings.com
- Moody's: www.moodys.com
- Standard & Poor's: www.standardandpoors.com

Understanding Insurance Jargon

What does *guaranteed renewable* mean? What about *evidence of insurability?* Go to www.investorwords.com for clear, easy-to-understand definitions.

Keeping Insurance Costs Low

- Comparison shop. Different insurance companies have different rate structures.
- Select a deductible as high as you can reasonably afford. It keeps premium costs down.
- Pay only for coverage you need. You may not need a Cadillac policy. Perhaps a Chevy will do.
- If possible, look into consolidating your policies. I get a discount on my auto and homeowner's policies because I have them with the same insurer.
- Take care of yourself. The healthier you are, the less you will tend to spend on many types of insurance.

Your Bottom Line

If you haven't figured out the types of insurance you need, think about your priorities, and do so now. Creating a plan for your insurance is an important part of your efforts to align your goals with your priorities. You should do this sooner rather than later.

Insurance payments are made in different ways, in different time frames, and it may take you some time to figure out the right policies that you need. For more information on all kinds of insurance, go to the Federal Citizen Information web site. As the name indicates, it's sponsored by the government. The URL is www.pueblo.gsa.gov.

Once you've determined the coverage that works best for you, determine how it affects your monthly budget, and insert that number into your Bottom Line.

CHAPTER

15

Investing for Your Future

Investing tends to shine a bright light on people's attitudes toward money. Some of my past clients come to mind:

- The volunteer fireman, a natural risk taker, who would have put all his money on the roulette wheel in Las Vegas if I'd told him to.
- The young, single professional who told me she never worried about her investments, but what she meant was they scared her so much that she couldn't bear to think about them.
- The corporate manager with a nest egg of $150,000 who wanted to withdraw $100,000 from it every year and wondered what kind of return he'd need. (The answer is about 66⅔ percent!)

All of them had past experiences that colored their attitudes toward money in general, and investing in particular.

It's Not Rocket Science

When someone talks to you about investing, does your mind just shut down? Are all the terms hopelessly confusing? Investing is not rocket science, though some of the articles you read might convince you of it. It's my opinion that many investment advisors *try* to confuse you, so that you won't ask too many questions. To make the right investing decisions you just need to know two things:

1. What's your time horizon?
2. What's your tolerance for risk?

199

And a few things about the world of investing:

- Types of investments.
- The importance of diversifying your portfolio.
- The kind of investments that work best for you.

The real truth is—the most complicated thing about investing is the vocabulary. So let's talk about some of the basic concepts of investing.

Time Horizon

Your *time horizon* is when you are going to need the money. This will help determine the types of things you should invest in.

Let's look at some of the ways in the ways in which your portfolio would likely change, based on your time horizon:

- If you have less than one year until you need your money, you will want to keep your money in cash equivalents—money market accounts, savings, and short-term certificates of deposit (CDs).
- If your time horizon is 1 to 5 years, most of your money should be in cash and short-term bonds.
- If your time horizon is 5 to 10 years, your money should be in cash, bonds, and perhaps some equity (stocks).
- If your time horizon is 10 years or more, you want a mix of stocks, bonds, and cash. The farther away your goal is, the more money you should have in stocks.

Risk

Most people don't like risk. And as we'll see below, when looked in a particular way, stocks are riskier than other investments. But looks can be deceiving (more on that in just a moment). Stocks are more volatile than bonds and cash. They have more variability in their returns, from one year to the next. But on average, their returns tend to be higher over the long run—large company stocks returned, on average, more than 10 percent per year in the 80-year period from 1925 to 2005. If you have all your money in a savings account in a bank, however, you won't have a lot of volatility, but your returns may barely keep up with inflation. (Once you pay taxes on your earnings, you might not even do that.) So there's a risk to cash as well. It's known as inflation or purchasing power risk. Bonds have a risk, too. The risk associated with them is that interest rates will change after you buy them. That's called interest rate risk, logically enough. You need to balance all these economic risks when you look at investments.

You also need to understand your own risk tolerance, and where it comes from. Does the stock market make you really nervous? If so, why? Is it because you don't know enough about it? Are you working off of gender scripts? Understanding your own tolerance for risk will help you to make the best investing decisions for you.

The New York Institute of Finance has an online risk quiz we like, which can be found at www.icief.org/risk/risk_quiz.html. Try it, and see where your risk tolerance falls.

Once you've learned something about risk tolerance, you'll be able to pick the investments that won't keep you up at night. There are mutual funds designed to take your risk tolerance into consideration. To illustrate the relationship between risk and return, we'll use the Vanguard LifeStrategy funds as an example.

Vanguard has four LifeStrategy funds. They are all hybrid funds; that is, they contain stocks, bonds and short-term investments. They are also funds-of-funds. That means they each have a bunch of Vanguard funds in them: the Vanguard Total Stock Market Index Fund, the Vanguard Total Bond Market Index Fund, the Vanguard Asset Allocation Fund, the Vanguard Total International Stock Index Fund, and the Vanguard Short-Term Investment-Grade Fund. Because they are designed for people with different risk tolerances, however, they each have those funds in different proportions.

The Vanguard LifeStrategy Growth Fund holds between 65 percent and 90 percent of its assets in stocks, between 10 percent and 35 percent in bonds, and between 0 and 25 percent in short-term fixed income investments. Over the five years to January 31, 2007, its average annual return was 9.21 percent. It lost 15.8 percent in 2002, a very bad year for stocks, and gained 16.1 percent in 2006, a very good year for stocks.

The Vanguard LifeStrategy Moderate Growth Fund holds between 45 percent and 70 percent of its assets in stocks, between 30 percent and 55 percent in bonds, and between 0 and 25 percent in short-term fixed income investments. Over the five years to January 31, 2007, its average annual return was 8.17 percent. It lost

10.3 percent in 2002, a very bad year for stocks, and gained 13.3 percent in 2006, a very good year for stocks.

The Vanguard LifeStrategy Conservative Growth Fund holds between 25 percent 50 percent of its assets in stocks, between 30 percent and 55 percent in bonds, and between 20 percent and 45 percent in short-term fixed income investments. Over the five years to January 31, 2007, its average annual return was 6.83 percent. It lost 5.4 percent in 2002, a very bad year for stocks, and gained 10.6 percent in 2006, a very good year for stocks.

The Vanguard LifeStrategy Income Fund holds between 5 percent and 30 percent of its assets in stocks, between 50 percent and 75 percent in bonds, and between 20 and 45 percent in short-term fixed income investments. Over the five years to January 31, 2007, its average annual return was 5.57 percent. It lost 0.1 percent in 2002, a very bad year for stocks, and gained 7.9 percent in 2006, a very good year for stocks (*Source:* vanguard.com).

Given the returns and the volatility of these funds, and considering your own risk tolerance, which do you think would work best for you?

There are plenty of tools on the market that allow you to honor your risk tolerance and work within your time horizon. As I said before, investing is not rocket science. Still, there are complex issues at work in our investment choices.

Your Scripts about Investing

What are the lessons you learned when you were growing up that affected your perceptions about investing? Was investing something left to the men in your family? Did your parents live through the Great Depression and develop a lasting fear of the stock market? Go to "Your Story" at the end of Chapter 6 and see if you noted any early messages about investing that are playing out in your financial behavior today. If you see any that don't work in your best interest, you are going to want to remember you have those tendencies when you make investment choices. Write them down.

Also enter FS (family script) in the designated column of your Bottom Line. That way, it can serve as a reminder on your way to making your goals a reality.

_____

_____

_____

Let's do the same thing with societal messages. Look at "Your Story" at the end of Chapter 5. Are any of the pressures to "keep up with the Joneses," follow gender scripts, or the stereotypes about investing for your race or ethnic group playing out in your behavior? Write them down if those messages are not bringing you closer to your goals. Also enter SS (societal script) in the designated column of your Bottom Line. That way, it can serve as a reminder as you make the financial choices that will make your goals a reality.

_____

_____

_____

_____

_____

What about the songs that are stuck in your head? Do one or more of these sound like you?

- I don't have time to think about investing.
- I don't know enough to make good investing decisions.
- Family members have made terrible investing decisions in the past; I don't want to imitate them.
- My spouse and I have such different opinions about investing that we avoid the issue entirely.
- I don't have enough money to invest.
- Any mention of the word _investing_ makes my eyes roll back into my head.

Write your messages down. Also put IS (internal script) in the designated column of your Bottom Line. That way, it can serve as a reminder on your way to making your goals a reality.

_____

_____

_____

_____

_____

If you've decided to make some changes to your investment planning, where do you think you are in the change process? Here are the six stages Dr. Prochaska and his colleagues identified and the abbreviations you should use on your Bottom Line, as you put that information onto the chart:

1. Precontemplation (PC)
2. Contemplation (C)
3. Preparation (P)
4. Action (A)
5. Maintenance (M)
6. Termination (T)

Review the techniques that will allow you to move out of that stage. Also, look at the notes you took on how to make each of the techniques work for you. You may want to jot some of those down, so that you can refer to them during this chapter. In addition, use the following abbreviations to note those change techniques in the "Technique" column on your Bottom Line:

- Consciousness raising (CR)
- Social liberation (SL)
- Emotional arousal (EA)
- Self-reevaluation (SR)
- Commitment (C)
- Countering (CT)
- Environment control (EC)
- Reward (R)
- Helping relationships (HR)

_____

_____

_____

_____

Types of Investments

Stocks

Stocks are shares of ownership in a company. Since crazy things can happen to any one company (think Enron), the best way for most people to own stock is though mutual funds. In fact, many planners I know do not put clients into individual stocks until their portfolios reach $5 million or more.

There are different types of stocks. There are growth stocks, which have a high price-to-earnings ratio. They are expected to grow quickly. There are value stocks, with a lower price to earnings ratio. The market looks at them as relative "bargain" stocks. There are blend stocks, which have elements of both growth and value. For the past few years, value has outperformed growth. In the late 1990s, growth outperformed value. Own both types, or a blend fund, and no matter which is currently in favor, in an up market for stocks your portfolio will perform.

Growth, value, and blend stocks can be large company (large cap), midsized company (midcap), and small company (small cap). They can be U.S. or foreign companies.

These different kinds of stocks react differently to changes in the financial markets. Large-company stocks tend to be more stable (less volatile). Small-company stocks tend to grow more quickly over time. Foreign stocks will perform well when the dollar is weak or when global events favor non-U.S. companies.

Large-company U.S. stocks and stock mutual funds are a basic component of a long-term portfolio, but all types of stock funds have a place in a diversified portfolio.

Bonds

Bonds are the debt of companies or governments. You can buy IBM bonds, New Jersey municipal bonds, or U.S. Treasury bills, bonds, or notes. You can buy investment-quality or high-yield (also known as junk) bonds. You can buy U.S. or foreign bonds. You can buy short-, intermediate-, or long-term bonds or bond funds.

Intermediate-term bonds and bond funds are a basic component of a long-term portfolio. For people in high tax brackets, municipal bonds and bond funds make sense for nonretirement monies. High-yield bond funds, when used as a small percentage of a diversified portfolio, can increase diversification and add return, as can global bonds.

Retirement portfolios, which need inflation protection, can benefit from a type of long-term government bonds called Treasury inflation-protected securities (TIPS), which have inflation protection built in.

Again, for most people, the best way to own these investments is in the form of mutual funds.

Cash

Cash is the one investment everyone understands. You can own cash in a mutual fund as a money-market mutual fund. Or you may have cash in your checking or savings account or in CDs.

Performance

We've talked about the different types of investments, now let's talk about performance.

Over the long term, stocks, particularly those of small companies, tend to outperform just about any other kind of investment. So why not just put all of your money into stocks? Because along with that return comes a lot of volatility. Most people have a hard time dealing with the ups and downs of the equities markets. Here's an example:

- On October 5, 1987, Microsoft stock closed at $73.50 per share.
- On October 26, 1987, it closed at $37.25 per share, a decline of 49 percent (*Source:* Yahoo! Finance).

Not knowing the future, would you have held it or sold it? Your grandmother knew the answer. Remember when she told you not to put all your eggs in one basket? Putting all of your money into one type of investment is not a good thing.

It's impossible to predict what's going to happen in the financial markets. No one could have predicted Hurricane Katrina and its effect on worldwide energy prices. That rise in prices got us more interested in energy conservation, and in my opinion, opened up the discussion about global warming and the environment.

How do you protect your investments against extraordinary events like Katrina? You diversify your portfolio. Having a mix of stocks, bonds, and cash will protect you in good times and bad. Which type of investment should you own? All of them. Each will perform differently in different market conditions. Over the past few years, foreign stocks have been the best-performing type of investment. But for a few years before that, bonds alternated as the market leaders with small company stocks. Before that, it was large U.S. companies. Some years, only cash does well.

There's a statistical way to look at the way these investments relate to one another. It's called *correlation*, literally co-relation. The correlation between stocks, bonds, and cash is very low and is sometimes negative. That's why you want to own all of them. No matter what happens to the financial markets, if you own all of these investments, chances are that part of your portfolio will be doing well. Financial planners call this building an uncorrelated portfolio.

If you build an uncorrelated, diversified portfolio, you will also tend to get more return for less risk, over time. The research behind this is called Modern Portfolio Theory, and won the Nobel Prize in economics in 1990 for its originators: Harry Markowitz, Merton Miller, and Bill Sharpe.

Other Investments

Stocks, bonds, and cash are not the only types of investments out there. You can buy commodities, like orange juice futures. You can buy real estate. You can invest in collectibles, like gold coins or antiques. Hedge funds and private equities are also very much in the news. Most of these things are available as mutual funds, but they tend to be quite volatile. Do they make sense for your portfolio? In small amounts, they may. Again, don't put all your eggs in any of these baskets.

That's All Very Interesting, but What Do I Do?

To put all this information into action, the best step is to take a look at where you are now.

If you want to see the different securities your mutual fund owns, or if you want to do research on mutual funds you might want to buy, go to www.morningstar.com and check your fund's Morningstar category. You want to own mutual funds from many different categories to keep your overall portfolio diversified.

Then you need to figure out what kind of asset allocation works for you. Any mutual fund company or discount brokerage Web site will give you a risk tolerance quiz and help build you an asset allocation. I like index funds, which simply match an index like the S&P 500, so my own personal money is at Vanguard, which is known for index funds. Using a mutual fund or discount broker is a matter of personal preference. No investment company is perfect, so it's important that you find one that suits your needs.

The most important thing to understand about buying mutual funds is their costs. Each fund has an expense ratio. That's what it costs to own it. Vanguard's Total Stock Market Index (VTSMX) is 19 basis points, or just less than one-fifth of 1 percent. Fidelity's Spartan Total Market Index Fund (FSTMX) is even cheaper—10 basis points, or one-tenth of 1 percent. Both funds use a passive or index strategy to mirror the performance of the entire U.S. stock market.

Actively managed funds are generally much more expensive. You can pay 100 basis points, or 1 percent per year to own such a fund. You can also pay much, much more.

More expensive is *not* better when it comes to mutual funds. There has been massive research on mutual funds, going back decades, and there is *no* relationship between added cost and increased performance.

Be careful of load funds. These are funds that have an extra cost, called a *load*, attached to them. They are generally sold through brokers. The load adds to the cost. The load can come when you buy it (front-end load), when you sell it (back-end load), or the entire time you own it (level load). Stacey and I, and most financial planners we know, buy only "no-load, no-transaction fee" funds.

How do you find out if you have a load fund? Visit www.morningstar.com or http://finance.yahoo.com/funds. Type in the fund's name or put in the ticker symbol, which is five letters long, ending in "x." There will be expense information about the fund.

(One note on load funds: You may have a fund in your company retirement plan that looks like a load fund. In other words, when you look it up, it says it has a load. These funds generally have "A" after the fund name. In most cases, the load is waived for retirement plans, and you do not have to pay it.)

Exchange-Traded Funds

There's been a lot of attention paid lately to exchange-traded funds (ETFs). For most of their history, ETFs tracked indexes, just as index mutual funds do. Now they are starting to be actively managed. Generally, they are low cost, which we like a lot. But they are a slightly different animal than mutual funds, and it's important to understand the differences.

ETFs are brokerage funds. There are costs involved both in buying and selling them. That means they don't work well for regular deposits. If you are saving $200 per month for your child's college, you probably don't want to do it in an ETF. You may want to use a mutual fund or other college savings option instead. If, however, you want to invest your annual bonus in an index fund, an ETF may make sense. They are good for periodic large purchases, where the brokerage costs do not matter so much. ETFs are also great for taxes. You don't pay tax until you sell the fund. In fact, most index funds have tax advantages.

Active versus Passive (Index) Management

One of the more amusing things I see when I go to investment conferences is the debate between active and passive managers. Active managers think active management is best. Well, *of course* they do. Passive managers feel exactly the same way. And here's the crux of the debate: Do you think it's possible for a human being to beat the market over the long term? If you do, you want your funds to be actively managed. If you don't, you want a passive index.

What If I Just Don't Want to Think about This?

There's a solution for you as well. It's called a *balanced fund*. It's a hybrid fund, with both stocks and bonds in it. A balanced fund will normally have a ratio of 60 percent stocks to 40 percent bonds. Make sure it has some international stocks. If not, add an international stock fund to your mix.

Another solution is a target date fund, already mentioned in Chapter 13. Target date funds are "funds of funds." Each fund has a number of funds in it, containing lots of different types of investments. Select the target date fund nearest your retirement date, and you will get a diversified portfolio that will become more conservative over time. Your money can even stay in the fund after you retire, since all of these funds become income-oriented 5 to 10 years after the target retirement date.

Your Bottom Line

You have already taken a look at your retirement and savings targets. If you have other monies available to invest, you can meet your goals sooner. What is the amount of cash you are able to invest each month? Add that amount to your Bottom Line.

Table 15.1   How Savings Grow over Time

Monthly Savings	5	10	20	30	40 Years at 7% Return
$100	$7,159	$17,308	$52,093	$121,997	$262,481
250	17,898	43,271	130,232	304,993	656,203
500	35,796	86,542	260,463	609,985	1,312,407
1,000	71,593	173,085	520,927	1,219,971	2,624,813
2,500	178,982	432,712	1,302,317	3,049,927	6,562,033
5,000	357,965	865,424	2,604,633	6,099,855	13,124,067

Table 15.1 shows how savings adds up over time.

You can factor this money into your long-term financial planning. You can add it to your retirement projections or education savings, or just know that it is going to be there to help you achieve your goals.

CHAPTER 16

The Real Cost of College

A financial services firm once aired a commercial that showed a premature baby in a hospital bed with all sorts of monitors attached to her, and her distraught father leaning over her. The doctor points out to the father that it will cost a fortune to send the child to college, and he should be glad she's premature, because that gives him more time to save up. This is shameful! It is much easier to send a child to college than the financial services industry would have us believe.

I'm not saying that the costs of a college education are not enormous—the numbers can prompt chest pains in the healthiest of parents, and we'll talk more about this in just a moment—but I am always surprised at the number of children and parents who do not use the numerous options for some form of financial aid.

For example, you are eligible for certain types of grants if you do community service, regardless of your financial background. What a great way to teach kids about philanthropy! Many internships offer education grants. There are grants available for those interested in various sectors of the medical field.

Life Planning opens up the idea that how your children's education gets paid for is part of their education. In addition, studies have shown that children take higher education much more seriously if they pay for a portion of it. Perhaps targeting a grant in an area of interest and working to fulfill its obligations would allow your children to make a financial contribution and teach them a lesson about the benefits of reaching their goals.

Think about the messages you would like to send your children about a college education and how you can use your finances to help reinforce those messages. You may decide that having them pay for part of their education will teach them to value it more. Encouraging them to work for grants and scholarships may seem like a great way to teach them to find creative ways to pay for the things they want to achieve. You may feel that they need to look at a college education as non-negotiable and want them to focus on school while you worry about the money.

Think about these things, and write some of your ideas down. Have a talk with your children about what they want to get out of their college experience. Does she want to go to Harvard because Elle Woods went to law school there in the movie *Legally Blonde*? Or does she want to take a political philosophy course with Michael Sandel because it's an area of consuming interest to her? Find out. It may affect your decision about the best way to fund your children's education.

_____

_____

_____

_____

_____

Life without Harvard

There is an abiding myth that the college a person attends determines with some degree of certainty his or her future success in life. This does not appear to be true. As Carol Hymowitz reported in the September 18, 2006, *Wall Street Journal:* "The college diplomas of the nation's top executives tell an intriguing story: Getting to the corner office has more to do with leadership talent and a drive for success than it does with having an undergraduate degree from a prestigious university."

It's perfectly normal to want your children to go to a "great" college. One of the most common things new parents tell me is that they plan on sending their kids to Harvard. But consider:

- For the 2006–2007 academic year, Harvard University's Web site listed tuition and fees at $43,655.
- The Rutgers University (one of New Jersey's state colleges) Web site listed tuition and fees for 2006–2007 at about $18,800, depending on housing and meal choices.
- Union County (New Jersey) College 2006–2007 tuition and fees were $3,516 for county residents for a typical year's workload. This does not including housing and meals because all students commute.

Some financially savvy friends have given their children these options:

- Four years at a state school or the equivalent anywhere, with the kids picking up the difference in scholarships and loans.
- Two years of community college and two years at any school.
- Associate degree at a community college only, with the kids financing the rest.
- A paid year abroad, while the kids help cover the education costs back at home. They helped to cover their end of the bargain by qualifying for grants and scholarships.

Think about your children's wants and needs, and the ways in which college costs will impact your total budget as you come up with the best options to finance their education. I've known people to do things like use their retirement money to pay for college. This ends up costing the entire family down the road—the parents need more financial assistance when they retire, which puts stress on everyone.

The Numbers

We calculated the future value of these cost of the colleges mentioned above. From there, we calculated the amount you'd have to save each month, so that you would have a guideline to calculate the monthly cost of your best course of action. We used the commonly cited 6 percent inflation rate for higher education and assumed a 7 percent tax-deferred return on your investments (see Table 16.1).

Based on what you know now, how much do you need to save? (You can always readjust this figure after you've established other financial assistance.) We'll fill your monthly savings allocation into your Bottom Line at the end of this chapter. You may learn some

Table 16.1 Future Cost of College

	Future Cost		Time until College ...			
	2006–2007	× 4 Years	5	10	15	20 Years at 6% Inflation
Harvard	$43,565	$174,260	$233,199	$312,073	$417,624	$558,875
Rutgers	18,800	75,200	100,635	134,672	180,221	241,177
Union County College	3,516	14,064	18,821	25,186	33,705	45,105

	Monthly Savings		Time until College ...			
	2006–2007	× 4 Years	5	10	15	20 Years at 7% Return
Harvard	$43,565	$174,260	$3,238	$1,793	$1,310	$1,067
Rutgers	18,800	75,200	1,397	774	565	460
Union County College	3,516	14,064	261	145	106	86

tips that may affect that number. For now, I just want you to have a general idea of what your monthly costs will be.

The Inside Story

Next, let's find out if there are any scripts in your past that have kept you from meeting your financial goals for this aspect of your savings. We want to see if you need to make some changes, so that you can apply the proper techniques at the right time.

Think about the following questions as we determine how the early messages you got about paying for education are affecting your actions today. Do you have a college education? If so, how did it get paid for? How do you think that affected your current attitudes about paying for college? Is this in line with your ideals? Is it playing out in your current financial behavior? Do you want to change this? Also, take a look at "Your Story" in Chapter 4. Did you note any scripts or behaviors that are affecting the way you save in general? If you think any of your early lessons are working against the way you want to contribute to your child's higher education expenses, write them down. Also put FS (family script) in the designated column of your Bottom Line, so that you'll be reminded of these tendencies when you do your overall financial planning.

_____

_____

_____

_____

_____

Let's do the same thing with societal messages. Look at "Your Story" at the end of Chapter 5. Are social pressures to "keep up with the Gateses," follow your gender scripts, or follow the scripting regarding your race or ethnic group affecting your savings in a way that is working against the contribution you want to make to your child's higher education expanses? Take some notes. Also put SS (societal script) in the designated column of your Bottom Line. That way, it can serve as a reminder on your way to making your goals a reality.

_____

_____

_____

_____

_____

What about the songs that are stuck in your head? What are they saying to you about your savings skills? Are any working against your goals for the money you want to give your child for higher education? Write them down. Also put MS (mental script) in the designated column of your Bottom Line.

_____

_____

_____

_____

_____

If you want to change the ways in which your savings behavior, specifically that regarding your child's education expenses, think about where you are in the change process. Again, here are the six stages Dr. Prochaska and his colleagues identified, and the abbreviations you should use on your Bottom Line, as you put that information onto the chart:

1. Precontemplation (PC)
2. Contemplation (C)
3. Preparation (P)
4. Action (A)
5. Maintenance (M)
6. Termination (T)

Review the techniques that will allow you to move out of that stage. Also, look at the notes you made on how you can make that technique work best for you. You may want to jot some of those down, so that you can refer to them during this chapter. In addition, use the following abbreviations to note those change techniques in the "Technique" column on your Bottom Line:

- Consciousness raising (CR)
- Social liberation (SL)
- Emotional arousal (EA)
- Self-reevaluation (SR)
- Commitment (C)
- Countering (CT)
- Environment control (EC)
- Reward (R)
- Helping relationships (HR)

_____

_____

_____

_____

_____

Financial Aid

I was once with a group of planners discussing this subject, and the conclusion we came to is that the best thing a parent could do is have quadruplets. They will all enter college in the same year, and since financial aid forms calculate the most a parent can possibly afford to spend on college, you can send four kids to school for the price of one.

Since most people don't plan for college by having quadruplets, we will look at some alternatives.

If you are considering financial aid, the poorer you are, the better. That's true for both you and your child. In addition, certain assets count more heavily in financial aid calculations.

The interplay between savings vehicles, which we will talk about later, and financial aid, is important:

- Anything that belongs to your child is more likely to be included by financial aid as available to pay for college expenses.
- Anything that belongs to you counts less.
- Anything that belongs to your child's grandparents does not count at all.

If you have money set aside for college in a number of different places, spend your child's money first. Spend yours second. And if there are grandparents who want to help, you will want to coordinate their contributions so that they do not interfere with your child's ability to obtain financial aid.

If you have credit card or other consumer loans, pay them off. It does not make sense to have money in your checking account that counts against you when you have loans outstanding.

If you are divorced, it may make sense for the parent with less income to take the child as a dependent on their tax return. That way they become the primary parent for the purposes of the financial aid application, and may qualify for more aid.

Applying for Financial Aid

To apply for student financial aid from the federal government, including the Pell Grant, Perkins Loan, Stafford Loan, and work-study, you will need to submit the Free Application for Federal Student Aid (FAFSA). There is no charge for submitting this form. The FAFSA is also required by all state and many school student assistance programs.

Some private colleges and universities will require one or more supplemental forms to obtain information not included on the FAFSA. They may have their own forms or they may ask you to complete the College Board's CSS PROFILE form. You can check out www.fafsa.ed.gov/for more information·

Scholarships

There are many scholarship sites on the Internet. Some are need based, but others are based on special qualities, affiliation, or talents your child has. Income is not always a determinant. Avoid those that charge you fees. Free Web sites that are mentioned by a number of financial Web sites and writers include:

- www.fastweb.com
- http://apps.collegeboard.com/cbsearch_ss/welcome.jsp
- www.scholarships.com

Also check with your local library for their search capabilities.

And if your child has an unusual interest, it makes sense to see what's out there. I happen to enjoy listening to bagpipes, and saw on the news the other day that Carnegie Mellon University offers a bag-pipe scholarship, but few people apply for it (see www.cbsnews.com/stories/2006/09/22/assignment_america/main2034805.shtml).

It doesn't have to be bagpipes. It could be harmonicas or lizards or nuclear physics or Renaissance art. Look up organizations cater-ing to people with your child's interest. Often, they offer scholar-ships. At the very least, your child could find a network that may be very useful in the future.

Grants

If you are a member of a minority group, there may be grant and scholarship assistance available to you.

- The organization A Better Chance lists a variety of resources. For some of its general college Web sites, see www.abetterchance.org/OtherResource/College/Gen_College5.html.
- And some specifically for Native Americans: www.abetterchance.org/ReferralOrgs&Resources/res-coll_native_schol1.htm
- One of the oldest organizations offering such help is the United Negro College Fund: www.uncf.org.
- The Hispanic Scholarship Fund has similar goals for its con-stituency: www.hsf.net.

Military Service.   The G.I. Bill has been recently enhanced to allow for greater educational assistance to veterans. Rates will depend on your years of service, whether you are full or part time, and how many dependents you have.

State Grants.   Each state is responsible for managing its educational grant programs. Many states have grants and scholarships based on merit, need, and even area of study.

Sallie Mae.   Sallie Mae, formerly a governmental entity, but now a private organization that provides student loans, offers some scholarship opportunities on its College Answer Web site: www.ollegeanswer. com/paying/content/pay_featured_scholarship.jsp.

Scholarships for Community Service

As I mentioned earlier in the chapter, there are also scholarships available for those who have performed, or who are willing to commit to perform, significant community service: www.finaid.org/otheraid/service.phtml.

Work-Study

Aside from the Federal Work-Study Program (www.ed.gov), which is part of many students' financial aid packages, other organizations offer their own plans. The U.S. Department of Housing and Urban Development, for example, has a Community Development Work Study Program to attract students to careers in community and economic development (www.hud.gov/progdesc/cdwsp.cfm).

Cooperative Education

Per Wikipedia, "Cooperative education is a structured method of combining academic education with practical work experience." The work experience is normally paid. Typically, a student takes five years to complete an undergraduate degree but has a significant amount of work experience by that time and has earned a competitive salary in his or her field while working. Engineering is a typical co-op field.

   For more information about co-op programs, take a look at the National Commission on Cooperative Education Web site,

www.co-op.edu, or the World Association for Cooperative Education Web site, www.waceinc.org.

Working for the Government

Does your child have an interest in public service? There's a Web site
that offers students to opportunity to work in the government: www.
studentjobs.gov.

Where to Save

It used to be that parents saving for college put money in a savings
account earmarked for the purpose. Now there are lots of options.

529 Plans

Section 529 plans are offered by each state. You can pick a plan from
any state; you are not limited to your own state's plan. Why use them?
You control the money if you set up the account, but it's out of your
estate and in your child's name. It does not, however, count against
your child for financial aid purposes. And—very important—although
you contribute the money after tax, the money builds tax free and
there are no taxes on distributions if used for qualified educational
expenses. Money can also be transferred among family members.

There are two kinds of 529 plans:

1. Prepaid tuition plans, where units of tuition are purchased for
    the future at today's prices.
2. Savings and investment plans, which are more like a savings
    account.

The most comprehensive source for information about these plans is
the College Savings Plans Network Web site: www.collegesavings.org.
The site was developed by the National Association of State Treasurers.

Once you have decided on the type of plan, the next step is to
decide which state's plan you want to use. Two things are important. The first is whether your state has a plan where your contributions are deductible for state income tax purposes. If you have high
state taxes, you'll want to think about that. The second is fees and
expenses. This issue is complicated, and I'm going to refer you to an
expense analyzer developed by the National Association of Securities

Dealers. But here's the key: All of these investments have expenses associated with them. These directly impact the return you get on your investments. The higher the expenses, the less money you will have at the end of the day, all other things being equal.

For the 529 Expense Analyzer, see http://apps.nasd.com/investor_ Information/Smart/529/Calc/529_Analyzer.asp.

Roth IRA

If you have a Roth IRA, which you are eligible for if your income is less than $110,000 (single) or $160,000 (married filing joint), you can withdraw contributions to pay for educational expenses. Earnings can be withdrawn tax free if you've had the account for at least five years and are over 59½.

Coverdell Education Savings Accounts

If your income is less than $110,000 per year, you may be able to establish a Coverdell account to pay for the qualified education expenses of your children. You can contribute $2,000 per year to a Coverdell account. Like the 529 plan, contributions are after tax but build tax free, and distributions are tax free if used for qualified educational expenses.

Custodial Accounts

These are the Uniform Gift to Minors Account (UGMA) and the Uniform Transfer to Minors Account (UTMA). They used to be one of the primary methods of transfer of money to children, but are less used today. The gifts are irrevocable, and they cannot be transferred among family members. They are also considered assets of the child and may impact his or her eligibility for financial aid.

Series EE and I Bonds

The federal government's Education Savings Bond program allows you to take a deduction for some or all of the interest you earn on savings bonds if you use the proceeds to pay for college expenses.

Savings bonds must be either Series EE/E or Series I bonds issued since 1990. In order to take the deduction, the bonds' principal and interest must be used to pay for qualified educational expenses in the year you cash in the bonds.

For the 2006 tax year, for single taxpayers, the tax exclusion for single filers is eliminated for income of $78,100 and above. For married taxpayers filing jointly, the tax exclusion is eliminated for income of $124,700 and above.

Hope and Lifetime Learning Credits

These are education credits available on your tax return. From IRS Publication 970:

Hope Credit

- Up to $1,500 credit per eligible student.
- Available only until the first two years of postsecondary education are completed.
- Available only for two years per eligible student.
- Student must be pursuing an undergraduate degree or other recognized educational credential.
- Student must be enrolled at least half time.

Lifetime Learning Credit

- Up to $2,000 credit per return.
- Available for all years of postsecondary education.
- Available for an unlimited number of years.
- Student does not need to be pursuing a degree.
- Available for one or more courses.

Both the Hope and Lifetime Learning credits are phased out for higher-income taxpayers. The credits are reduced for single filers with income between $43,000 and $53,000 and for married taxpayers earning $87,000 to $107,000 in 2006.

Loans

Loans fall into two main categories:

1. Student
2. Parent

The student loans can be either federal (Stafford and Perkins) or private. Federal parent loans are known as PLUS loans. There's a wealth of information about these on the Sallie Mae Web site: www.salliemae.com.

The two most important things to know about any loan are (1) terms and (2) interest rate. You want the most flexible possible payment schedule and the lowest possible rate.

We think that, for most families, student loans make the most sense. It's a great idea to send your child out into the world without debt, but not if it means that you will be depending on him or her later in life because you haven't had a chance to build assets yourself.

Save for Your Own Retirement First

We touched on this earlier in the chapter. There are many reasons to put your retirement savings first. For starters, many financial aid formulas do not include retirement assets in their formulas. So by saving for retirement, you are not jeopardizing your child's chance to get financial aid. And, as we mentioned earlier, using all your money to pay for college for the kids may mean that you are a burden on them later in life. Do you want that?

Your Bottom Line

Before you fill in an amount in your Bottom Line, ask yourself a few questions:

- Have you had a good conversation with your child(ren) about what college scenario makes sense?
- Are all family members on board?
- Have you done enough research on available options, including scholarships, grants and loans?

If so, let's revisit Table 16.1 we looked at in the first part of the chapter, using the three colleges on our example.

- What scenario and time horizon works for you and your family?
- Put that number in your Bottom Line.

CHAPTER 17

Giving Back

In Part I, you and Stacey looked at some of the beliefs and scripts that contribute to our fears about money. Remember Lynne Twist's "Three Myths of Scarcity" from Chapter 5?

Myth 1: There's not enough to go around.

Myth 2: More is better.

Myth 3: That's just the way it is . . . there are haves and have-nots.

In addition, we tend to associate money with security and protection, despite some of the awful things we've seen happen to really rich people. Combine these fears, insecurities, and the way the myths play out in many of our behaviors, and it's easy to see why a lot of people have a hard time parting with their money for anything other than their own needs.

But then, there's human nature: That part of the human spirit that inspires people to run into burning buildings to help others, without a second thought to their own safety. That part of the human spirit that prompted Americans to give $260.3 billion to charity in 2005 (according to Giving USA). That part of the human spirit that raised $3.5 billion for the relief efforts for hurricanes Katrina and Rita (as of February 20, 2006, according the Center on Philanthropy at Indiana University).

There's no charity in the world that doesn't benefit from money. You should give as much as you think you can, and then give a little more. You can also, however, make equally significant contributions with your time. There are even some unique opportunities to reap benefits in your personal finances from your philanthropic efforts. We're going to discuss unique ways you can allow your charitable giving to make the grandest statement of who you really are.

You Reap What You Sow

Think about a person whom you consider to be very generous. I'll bet all sorts of good feelings come up about them. I'll bet you wish them well and wish them a lot of happiness. People like generous people. Those with charitable natures tend to be rewarded for their efforts. They create a lot of goodwill in their own lives—a positive side effect, not the primary motivation, for their bighearted behavior.

Now think about people who let greed and fear guide their financial choices. Over the past few years, we've seen many in the corporate world who fall into this category being marched off to jail and stripped of the very fortunes they worked so hard to hold on to.

Life Planners like to talk about money as an energy that needs to flow. Choke it off, and at some point the levee will break. Have you ever seen a happy hoarder? As we discussed, humans are born with a giving nature, and trying to fool nature rarely works out well. Some of life's lessons may make us forget, but generosity is a core part of our being. This is one of the many reasons it's so important to stay connected to our inner values. Let them guide your financial choices, and you will be rewarded with good feelings and goodwill that is priceless!

Your Scripts about Philanthropy

Many planners cite the fact that some of their clients don't know how to allocate resources for philanthropy. Money is so rarely talked about that there aren't that many models of giving out there. Again, we're going to give you some ideas for this aspect of your finances, but first let's find out if there are any scripts at work that are affecting this part of your financial behavior.

What did you see in your family when it came to charitable giving? Do your early lessons support what you want to do with this aspect of your finances? Do they work against your personal beliefs? Would your financial behavior change if you were living in step with your values? Take some notes, and write them down. See if you put anything in "Your Story" at the end of Chapter 4 that may be having an impact on your philanthropic efforts. Put FS (family script) in the designated column of your Bottom Line if there are family messages you need to watch out for in your efforts to live in sync with your beliefs.

_____

_____

_____

_____

_____

    A society that believes it's important to "keep up with the Joneses" may not create the motivation we need to do all that we can when it comes to charity. In addition, ask people about philanthropy, and you'll notice that many seem to think it is something that only rich people do. Beliefs can also be at work in ethnic and racial stereotypes that may be affecting your behavior. Look at "Your Story" at the end of Chapter 5. Do you notice any attitudes or behaviors that are inconsistent with your core beliefs about charity? Write them down. Put SS (societal script) in the designated column of your Bottom Line.

_____

_____

_____

_____

_____

    Many of the tunes we sing to ourselves are rooted in fear: "If I give to others, I won't have enough for myself." "Other people will take care of those in need." What songs start playing when you think about charity? Write them down. Take a look at "Your Story" at the end of Chapter 6. If you notice any internal messages that may be drowning out your true beliefs and values, you'll want to note this on your Bottom Line. Put IS (internal script) in the designated column.

_____

_____

_____

_____

_____

Your Charitable Goals

Next, think about the grandest vision you have for yourself when it comes to charity. Here are a few questions to get you started:

- How would you like to be remembered?
- Are you giving as much to charity as you would like?
- Is the money you are giving doing the most possible good?
- Are you able to find a way to reach your own personal goals and still give back to the world?

Next, Stacey and I would like to know which charities and causes tug at your heartstrings. And we're not talking about the ones you feel a sense of obligation to, but the ones that would give you great happiness to help. List them here:

_____

_____

_____

_____

If you've decided to make some changes to the financial side of your charitable giving, where do you think you are in the change process that you worked on in Chapter 9? Again, here are the six stages Dr. Prochaska and his colleagues identified, and the abbreviations you should use on your Bottom Line, as you put that information onto the chart:

1. Precontemplation (PC)
2. Contemplation (C)
3. Preparation (P)
4. Action (A)
5. Maintenance (M)
6. Termination (T)

Review the techniques that will allow you to move out of that stage. Also, look at the notes you made on how you can make that technique work best for you. You may want to jot some of those down, so that you can refer to them during this chapter. In addition, use the following abbreviations to note those change techniques in the "Technique" column on your Bottom Line:

- Consciousness raising (CR)
- Social liberation (SL)
- Emotional arousal (EA)
- Self-reevaluation (SR)
- Commitment (C)
- Countering (CT)
- Environment control (EC)
- Reward (R)
- Helping relationships (HR)

_____

_____

_____

_____

_____

How to Give

My sister-in-law, Joan Smith Myers, who is director of development at the Peck School in New Jersey, often talks about how charitable giving has changed over the years. People used to just be content writing checks. Now they want accountability and a voice in how their money is spent.

If you know and love your charity, and all that they need is a check from you, this may still be a good option. But there are other ways to give.

Giving Time

There are many organizations today that run more on people than on money. Two of my cats came from the Summit Animal Rescue Association (SARA). Although SARA loves donations, they also desperately need foster parents and people to staff their tables at the local pet store, where they have cats available for adoption.

Cats not your thing? Mo, one of my work colleagues, spends one day a month at a food bank, putting food boxes together for families who need a bit of help. My friend Carolyn is a dynamite volunteer fund-raiser for our old school. She's quite soft-spoken, but she will not let our classmates off the phone until they give her a pledge.

What are your unique talents? There's always something you can do, from stuffing envelopes to organizing a book sale, to driving people to appointments, to helping create a marketing campaign.

If you're not sure where to start, Volunteer Match (www. volunteermatch.org) may be able to help. They connect people interested in volunteering with opportunities all over the country.

Giving Things

Your 1990 Ford Escort station wagon is not worth $5,000 as a charitable donation, even if you've kept it wrapped in tissue paper in a heated garage. In excellent condition, driven 80,000 miles, it's worth about $2,000 retail, according to the Kelley Blue Book (www.kbb.com).

Subject to certain limits, which we will talk about later, you can deduct the fair market value of items you donate to a qualified charity. Knowing the fair market value is important. People tend to overvalue big items and those with sentimental value and undervalue clothes. For clothes, by the way, the Salvation Army has an easy-to-use chart on one of its Web sites: www.salvationarmysouth. org/valueguide.htm.

You can also give financial securities like stocks and bonds. You can get fair market values at Web sites such as Yahoo! Finance: http://finance.yahoo.com/.

For heirlooms and collectibles, it's best to consult a professional appraiser. You can find one through the American Society of Appraisers (www.appraisers.org). Perhaps you'll have one of those great *Antiques Roadshow* moments and find out that the hideous bowl your Aunt Myra left you is from the Tang Dynasty.

Real Purchasing Power

Buying goods from organizations that donate a percentage of their profits to charities you support is a great way to make the most of your money. The American Heart Association has "Shop Go Red" (http://saturn.igetsmart.com/servlet/loaddaemon?Type=92& Load=ahawomen06&Field1=60186&Field2=0&Field3=0&Field4= 0&Field5=1).

You can buy things that raise money to fight:

- Breast cancer: http://shop.thebreastcancersite.com
- Hunger: www.thehungersite.com
- Illiteracy: www.theliteracysite.com

Raising Your Social Consciousness

Socially conscious or socially responsible investing allows you to put your money where your values are. You can buy stocks in companies whose goals you support. There are also mutual funds designed to follow certain social screens. The Ave Maria Funds follow Catholic values; the Amana Funds, Islamic ones. Many funds follow more general screens like good corporate governance or no tobacco or no weapons or environmental friendliness. There are even social index funds. My favorite, because of the name, is the Vanguard FTSE (pronounced "footsie") 4 Good Social Index Fund.

The Social Investment Forum (www.socialinvest.org), a not-for-profit organization, offers you a Web site to help you screen these funds according to your preferences.

Lending Money Charitably

There are more direct ways to get involved as well. An organization Stacey and I are familiar with, Shared Interest (www.sharedinterest.com), allows individuals to make loans that unlock credit for low-income communities in South Africa. The loaned money becomes part of a "guarantee fund." The fund's guarantees enable banks in South Africa to make loans to populations that might otherwise be considered too risky. Through what Donna Katzin, the founding executive director, calls a "multiplier effect," a $3,000 loan by an individual in the United States could result in tens of thousands of dollars of loans made in South Africa. A loan made to Shared Interest receives interest payments similar to what is paid on U.S. government bonds, and investors donate a portion of the interest back to the charity. This donated interest can be deducted as a charitable contribution. Since Shared Interest was established in 1994, it has benefited nearly a million black South Africans.

Community Foundations

Community foundations are tax-exempt charities focused on improving the quality of life in a certain geographic area. Your community needn't be large to have one. My own small town, Fanwood (and yes, there are small towns in New Jersey), has its own foundation.

If you would like to direct your charitable foundations toward your own community, here's a community foundation locator from the Council on Foundations (www.cof.org/Locator/).

Giving Circles

A Giving Circle is a pooled fund, normally hosted or sponsored by a charitable organization, through which members make charitable gifts as a group. This can be a great way to get together with people who share a common interest. To start or join one, talk to your favorite charity, or go to www.givingforum.org/givingcircles/downloads/Giving%20Circle%20Starter%20Kit.pdf.

Donor-Advised Funds

These are charitable funds in which the donor contributes cash or assets like stock to a sponsoring organization. As a planner, I see them set up when people have gotten a windfall, like an inheritance or a large bonus. They are also used by people who have written a lot of checks to charity, and now want to take a more systematic approach.

Very high net worth families normally do not take this route, but instead set up a more complex structure like a family foundation.

Four important things to know:

1. Your name or a name you choose, is on the fund (e.g., the Stacey F. Tisdale Foundation).
2. The donor gets a charitable contribution in the year that he or she contributes the assets.
3. The donor maintains some say in how the money is spent by making "grants."
4. The funds normally require a minimum initial investment of $10,000.

Where to find donor-advised funds? There are basically four places to go to set one up:

1. *A community foundation* (discussed above).
2. *A charity or not-for profit.* Your college probably has one, as do all the major foundations.

3. *An investment company.* Fidelity is probably the best known (in no small part due to the fact that its Web site URL is www.charitablegift.org), but T. Rowe Price, Vanguard, Schwab, and many other investment houses will set them up as well.
4. *Independent sponsors.* The American Endowment Foundation (www.aefonline.org) is the one most frequently mentioned.

If a donor-advised fund interests you, here are some questions to ask the sponsoring organization:

- What is your minimum contribution?
- How will the money be invested? Do I make that decision or do you?
- What services do you provide?
- What types of assets do you accept?
- What kinds of restrictions/limits do you place on grants?
- What is the minimum grant amount?

Charitable Trusts

Charitable Remainder Trust

This is a type of trust that's been around for a long time. Let's say you have a charity and you want to leave something to that charity in your estate. You also need income while you're alive. You set up a trust, put assets into it, and then, it's just like the words say: the charity gets the remainder, and you (or your beneficiaries) use the assets for income. You avoid capital gains tax on the assets you contribute, and get a charitable deduction for the fair market value of the remainder interest. And assets are no longer in your estate. One thing to note: The contribution is irrevocable—you can't change your mind later.

There are three main types of charitable remainder trusts:

1. *Charitable remainder annuity trust.* These pay a fixed amount each year.
2. *Charitable remainder unitrust.* This pays a percentage of the trust's value annually.
3. *Charitable pooled income fund.* This is a shared account with many others that pays you income.

Charitable Lead Trust

This is the reverse of a charitable remainder trust. You set up the trust and put assets into it. The charity gets income, and your heirs get the assets after you die.

Both charitable lead trusts and charitable remainder trusts are estate-planning tools. They should be part of your larger estate plan and should be discussed with your attorney.

Making Every Dollar Count

If you are giving your money locally, you can see how and where it is spent. But what if you want to give your money to a charity operating far away? It's harder to see what happens to your contribution. Hurricane Katrina taught us some rather scary lessons about some of the ways charities use money less than wisely.

The following resources can help you determine how your charity uses its money.

GuideStar

Philanthropic Research Inc.'s GuideStar Web site (www.guidestar.org) is a leading source for charitable information. It contains detailed information like the IRS Form 990s that charities must file with the government.

One of the interesting things about the site is that charities use it as frequently as donors. One can subscribe to the Web site at different levels. If you are just seeking basic information about a charity, you can register at no cost.

Better Business Bureau Wise Giving Alliance

The Better Business Bureau Wise Giving Alliance has published Standards for Charity Accountability. Organizations that comply with these accountability standards have provided documentation that they meet basic standards:

- In how they govern their organization
- In the ways they spend their money
- In the truthfulness of their representations
- In their willingness to disclose basic information to the public

Reports on whether organizations meet these standards are available at www.give.org.

Charity Navigator

Charity Navigator (www.charitynavigator.org) rates charitable organizations by organization efficiency and organizational capacity.

Giving and Taxes

IRS Tax Tip 2006-57 (www.irs.gov)

- You cannot deduct contributions made to specific individuals, political organizations, and candidates. Nor can you deduct the value of your time or services and the cost of raffles, bingo, or other games of chance.
- To be deductible, contributions must be made to qualified organizations.
- Only contributions actually made during the tax year are deductible.
- If your contributions entitle you to merchandise, goods or services, including admission to a charity ball, banquet, theatrical performance or sporting event, you can deduct only the amount that exceeds the fair market value of the benefit received.
- Donations of stock or other property are usually valued at the fair market value of the property.
- Special rules apply to donation of vehicles.
- For a charitable contribution of $250 or more, you can claim a deduction only if you obtain a written acknowledgment from the qualified organization.
- If you claim a deduction on your return of more than $500 for all contributed property, you must attach IRS Form 8283, Noncash Charitable Contributions, to your return.
- Taxpayers donating an item or a group of similar items valued at more than $5,000 must also complete Section B of Form 8283, which requires an appraisal by a qualified appraiser.

For more information, check out Publication 526, Charitable Contributions, which is available at www.irs.gov or by calling 1-800-TAX-FORM (1-800-829-3676).

Your Bottom Line

As you've seen, there are some unique ways to make financial and time commitments to charities that can help you live in sync with your personal values and still think about your personal financial goals.

Figure out how you can make contributions that reflect who you really are. Take a look at the charities you would like to give to, and think about the amount you can give financially. Determine the monthly amount you need to save, and reflect that number on your Bottom Line.

If the ways in which you choose to contribute come with a tax break or an interest payment, you can allocate that money toward you goals when you receive it. Use some of it to reward yourself for your generosity!

CHAPTER

18

Estate Planning

As you've journeyed through this book, you've been thinking a lot about your life stories. Now we'd like you to think about the story that will best reflect who you really are once you pass on. Are you the grandparent who always wanted to make sure your grandchildren were educated? Are you the parent who wouldn't want your children to worry about financial issues while they are grieving your loss? Are you the humanitarian who doesn't think the government and society do enough to help underprivileged children? Maybe the thought that "you can't take it with you" makes you want to spend it all now, and just make provisions for your burial costs. These are the types of things you may want to be reflected in your estate planning.

It used to be difficult to get people to talk about death. Then 9/11 happened. Suddenly, it became clear to everyone that life can be taken from us in an instant.

That reality means there are some questions we need to think about:

- Do you have a will?
- Do you have the other documents you need, like a living will?
- Have you kept your beneficiary designations up to date?
- If you were to die tomorrow, would your loved ones be cared for according to your wishes?
- If not, why?

The Messages You've Received about Estate Planning

Stacey once told me about a woman in her 50s that she knows, who is very concerned about her elderly parents' refusal to talk or think about estate planning. What Stacey found ironic was that the woman had not done any estate planning of her own. It's quite common for our ideals about this aspect of our finances to be overshadowed by the messages we received when we were growing up. Think about the legacy you want to leave behind. Think about why it's important. Is your financial behavior consistent with your beliefs? Take a look at "Your Story" at the end of Chapter 4. Are their any messages that are playing out in your estate planning that do not represent your values? If so, you'll want to bring this tendency into your awareness as you do your financial planning. Take some notes, and put FS (family scripts) in the designated space in your Bottom Line.

_____

_____

_____

_____

_____

Death is not a topic that society encourages us to talk about. In addition, we are so focused on our material lives that we tend to neglect planning for the ways in which we want our values to impact society after we've moved on. Gender messages—particularly those that tell women to stay out of financial planning—and stereotypes about race and ethnicity can play into our estate planning decisions as well. Look at "Your Story" at the end of Chapter 5 to help you determine if there are any societal scripts at work in your actions regarding estate planning. Take some notes, and put SS in the space designated for scripts in the legacy row of your Bottom Line if you have messages that may be preventing you from honoring your ideals.

_____

_____

_____

_____

What about those little voices that sing in your head? What tunes do they sing when you think about estate planning? "I'm never going to die." "I won't be here to worry about it." "I'll think about this later." Those songs may be inconsistent with your core beliefs but may still be playing out in your behavior. Take some notes, and put IS (internal script) in the designated "Scripts" column of your Bottom Line if you tend to act in a way that is inconsistent with your true estate-planning goals.

———————————————————————————

———————————————————————————

———————————————————————————

———————————————————————————

———————————————————————————

If you've decided to make some changes to the financial side of your estate planning, where do you think you are in the change process? Review the six stages Dr. Prochaska and his colleagues identified, and use the following abbreviations in the designated column of your Bottom Line:

1. Precontemplation (PC)
2. Contemplation (C)
3. Preparation (P)
4. Action (A)
5. Maintenance (M)
6. Termination (T)

Review the techniques that will allow you to move out of that stage. Also, look at the notes you took on how to make each of the techniques work for you. You may want to jot some of those down, so that you can refer to them during this chapter. In addition, use the following abbreviations to note those change techniques in the "Technique" column on your Bottom Line:

- Consciousness raising (CR)
- Social liberation (SL)
- Emotional arousal (EA)
- Self-reevaluation (SR)
- Commitment (C)

- Countering (CT)
- Environment control (EC)
- Reward (R)
- Helping relationships (HR)

_____

_____

_____

_____

_____

The Basics of Estate Planning

Estate planning can be very complicated. There are more kinds of trusts than you can shake a stick at, and many of them use strange rules and obscure IRS tables. We will describe a few kinds of common trusts, but we are going to leave the complicated stuff to your friendly neighborhood trusts and estates attorney.

One Thing that Confuses Everybody

Your will is important, but it does *not* control all your assets. For some things, like trusts, employee benefits and insurance policies, it *does not matter* what the will says. What controls how the assets are distributed is the beneficiary designation form. If you own property by either joint tenancy with right of survivorship, or tenancy by the entirety, the will won't control how that asset passes, either. The other owner gets it by law. And if you have assets in a trust, that passes outside the will as well.

Everything else is controlled by your will, and when you die, the will goes through probate, from the Latin for "prove." The probate process "proves" that the will is valid. If you do not have a will, your estate goes through an administrative process instead.

You Need a Will

Every adult American needs a will. If you don't have one, when you die you will be intestate (without a will), and the state in which you reside will determine how many of your assets are distributed. It varies from state to state, but generally this means that your assets go to your parents if you are not married and have no children, to your children if you are unmarried and have children, to your spouse if you are married with no children, and are split between your spouse and children if you are married with children. There may also be strings and stipulations attached to the assets, especially if you have children, and the people making the decisions about your assets may not be related to you in any way. Speaking as someone who has heard quite a few horror stories about intestacy, you do not want this.

Name Guardians for Minor Children in Your Will.   I once worked with the maternal grandparents of two young children whose parents had been killed in an accident. They had left no provision for guardians for the children. Relationships among the family members and in-laws were not good, and many years of expensive litigation resulted, leaving the assets of all the parties exhausted and the children being shuttled from one home to another. You do not want this for your family.

I do understand that you and your spouse may not agree on who makes the best guardian for your children. So it may make sense for you to switch named guardians every few years. Let your spouse have a pick, then you have a pick. Life is about compromise.

Make Sure Your Beneficiary Designations Are Up-to-Date.   A couple of years ago, I was brainstorming with a group of human resource managers about how to motivate employees to update their beneficiary designations. We came up with the following slogan: "Want to Make Your Ex Happy? *Don't* Update Your Beneficiary Designations!" There are a lot of happy exes out there. Employees tend to do these forms once, then forget about them. And then life happens.

Stacey and I think February is a great time to check, because an updated beneficiary designation form is the best Valentine's Day gift you can give the people you love.

Other Things to Consider

At some point in your life, you may need someone to speak for you if you cannot speak for yourself. Terry Schiavo taught all of us that. Here's some information about a few important forms:

Powers of Attorney

- A power of attorney is a legal document that allows a person (called the principal) to appoint another person (called the agent or attorney-in-fact) to act on his or her behalf. What powers this agent has should be explained in detail in the document. They can be specific or very general.

- When you sign a power of attorney, you do not give up your own right to act. What you are doing is making sure that your agent will be able to act when and how you have directed, if it becomes necessary.
- You need to trust the person you name as your agent completely, and you need to make sure that person is capable of performing the job. Ask the person if he or she is willing to take on the responsibility.
- When making these decisions, talk to your trusts and estates attorney.

Planning Your Medical Care and Treatment—Advance Directives. Advance directives are written documents that tell medical professionals what kind of treatment you do and don't want if you are unable to tell them yourself.

They can take many forms, and the laws about them are controlled by the state, not the federal government. Typing the words *advance directive* and the name of your state into an Internet search engine should bring you to the appropriate state agency and forms, but you should involve your trusts and estates attorney as well.

Federal law requires hospitals, nursing homes, and other institutions that receive Medicare or Medicaid funds to provide written information regarding advanced care directives to all patients upon admission.

Living wills are a kind of advance directive that comes into effect when a person is terminally ill. A living will allows you to specify the kind of treatment you want in a given situation.

A durable power of attorney for health care (sometimes called a durable medical power of attorney) gives a person you specify the ability to make medical decisions for you when you cannot. In most states, this cannot be one of your medical providers. Like other powers of attorney, you want to name someone who you trust deeply, who is willing to speak on your behalf, and who is wiling to make tough decisions and deal with possible conflicts among your family members when those decisions are made.

Trusts.   If you do not want to transfer property to another person outright, you can put it in a trust. There are hundreds of different kinds of trusts for all kinds of purposes, but you can put all of them into two types:

1. Living trusts are created while you are alive.
2. Testamentary trusts are created by your will.

These two kinds of trusts can either be irrevocable (you can't change them) or revocable (you can change them).

Why would you want to set up a trust? Living trusts are frequently set up to avoid probate. People who own property in a state with a complicated probate process may want to use one, as might people who own property in several different states. A living trust won't get you out of estate taxes, by the way. Many people think it can. But its purpose is to keep property out of probate. The IRS will still "see" it.

Testamentary trusts are frequently set up to take maximum advantage of the tax code. One common trust with married couples is a credit shelter (also know as a "bypass") trust. You can transfer all the assets you want to a spouse at your death with no taxes. If you do that, however, you don't take advantage of your uniform credit, which allows you to give $2 million (in 2007) to anyone you want without paying taxes. So, if you have a lot of money, you can put $2 million into a credit shelter trust and give your spouse the rights to the money while he or she is alive. After your spouse dies, the money in your credit shelter trust can go to your heirs, and your spouse can leave another $2 million (or whatever the amount is in that year) to them as well.

Trusts are a complicated business and not for the faint of heart. Ignore advice from friends, TV commercials, and personal finance pundits over whether or not you should set up a trust. Talk instead to a trusts and estates attorney about your own situation.

For more about trusts, visit the American Bar Association Web site: www.abanet.org/rppt/public/intro-to-wills.html#notgoverned.

Taxes

According to the IRS, only about 2 percent of estates are subject to federal estate tax (*Source:* www.irs.gov). Just for the record, though, Table 18.1 is what the estate tax table looks like.

State death taxes vary tremendously. If you are curious about your state's rules, the tax research company, CCH, has a guide, which can be found at www.finance.cch.com/text/c50s15d170.asp.

Table 18.1   Estate Tax Phaseout

The federal government's tax window closes over the next decade as the top estate-tax rate drops and the amount each person can pass free of federal estate taxes increases. The tax expires in 2010, though possibly for just one year.

Calendar Year	Exemption	Highest Rate
2002	$1 million	50%
2003	1 million	49
2004	1.5 million	48
2005	1.5 million	47
2006	2 million	46
2007	2 million	45
2008	2 million	45
2009	3.5 million	45
2010	Repealed	0
2011	1 million	55

Source: www.irs.gov

Finding a Trusts and Estates Attorney

The American Bar Association has links to resources for attorneys in your state (www.abanet.org/legalservices/findlegalhelp/home. cfm). For the purposes of this chapter, you would want an attorney who specializes in trusts and estates.

Your Bottom Line

Planning your estate is an important part of aligning your finances with your priorities. We urge you to know where you are in the change process, and the techniques that will help you make adjustments in this part of your financial planning if it does not represent the legacy you want to leave behind. Once you've done this, make the necessary adjustments to your Bottom Line.

CHAPTER

19

A Final Thought on Your Finances

You now have the financial blueprint for a life in which your most important goals and dreams, as well as your values, are a part of your everyday reality.

Your goals may change and your finances may change. Once you get out of debt, for example, you will have even more money for your other priorities. That's why we recommend that you update this chart at least once a month. (Stacey will talk more about that in Part III). In addition, we suggest you keep a copy of your Bottom Line in a place where you will see it at least once a day.

I asked you to do a lot in Part II, and I truly appreciate your effort. I wish you great luck as you live out a life that reflects who you really are!

PART III

STAYING ON COURSE

"You are already perfect. If you are not perfect, it is due to the poverty of your understanding. Get rid of this understanding and you will become rich. . . ."
—Swami Muktananda, *From the Finite to the Infinite*
(South Fallsburg, N.Y.: Siddha Yoga Publications, 1994)

CHAPTER 20

Staying on Course

So, how have things changed since we were sitting down at Starbucks in Chapter 1? You've been on quite a journey. Not only have you discovered the changes in your financial behavior that will make your goals a reality, but you have also transformed the beliefs and attitudes that were standing in your way.

This was no easy task. Those beliefs and attitudes run deep. They are connected to our family values, our community values, and our notions of right and wrong. Taking an honest look at those forces, and challenging those ideals that don't stand up to your inner wisdom, was a courageous endeavor. We commend you on your tremendous efforts!

No matter how deeply you choose to delve into this process, you will find that some of your perceptions about money have changed. Life Planning illustrates to even those who just skim the surface that there is more to our financial choices than just dollars and cents. That alone prompts a big transformation in the attitudes of many. But you bought this book because you wanted to make some changes to your financial behavior, and you've taken steps to make those changes real. Now you must maintain them in your everyday life.

The Honeymoon's Over

For a time, your new financial behavior is going to make things exciting. You'll be moving closer to your goals. You'll have new experiences because you're behaving differently. The people around you will take note and praise your efforts. During this period, it's almost like you're on cruise control. Momentum will carry you far and fast.

After a time, however, things will slow down. The "new you" becomes old news to your friends, family, colleagues, and even yourself. You will no longer be able to count on that excitement for motivation. This is why maintenance is one of the most challenging stages of the change process. You must find the tools within yourself to sustain your new behaviors.

It is important to remember, however, that maintenance is also the phase in which your new behaviors start to become first nature. Old habits and attitudes will fade from the forefront.

Change happens despite the barriers and defenses we try to throw in its way. Maintenance is about taking ownership of your new life and your new behaviors. It's about your creating the mental and physical environment in which transformation can occur.

Will Power

Before we look at techniques that will help you maintain your new behaviors, please try this exercise.

Exercise

- Go to a quiet place and get yourself situated in a comfortable seated position.
- Sit in a chair with your feet flat on the floor and hip-width apart. Sit forward so that your lower back does not round and slump. You may want to put a small cushion between your back and the back of the chair. Fold your palms in your lap with the back of right hand resting in the left palm. You can also touch your thumb and forefinger, and rest them on your thighs.
- Let your head relax and rise up in line with your spine. Relax your eyelids, cheeks, tongue, and the space between your eyebrows. Take a moment and just relax. Bring your attention to your breath.
- Think about a situation or a person that brings up intense feelings—maybe grief, anger, fear, pride, desire, and so on. If you can't think of a person or situation in your current life, use your memory to bring up an experience.

(Continued)

- Don't hold back—really let yourself feel these feelings. Visualize the person or situation that triggered them. What thoughts come up? How does it physically feel? Do you feel tightness in your stomach? Your head? Your heart?
- Now bring your full attention to those feelings. The person or situation that you used to spark these emotions will fade from the forefront. Let this happen. Let go of the story line, the person, and the drama. Let go of the thoughts that came up. Just focus on the physical feelings.
- Now give them up. Just let those feelings go. They are still inside, but don't give them any more attention. Bring your focus back to your breath.
- Do it again. Think of that situation or person. Really connect with the feelings and thoughts that come up. Let go of the situation. Let go of the thoughts and feelings.

What did you just do? You gave a situation power over your thoughts and emotions by giving it your full attention. Then you used your attention to take that power away.

It is incredibly easy to forget we have this ability in our "bag of tricks" when our various beliefs, habits, emotions, and thoughts are captivating our attention. These are some incredibly powerful forces.

As this exercise illustrated, however, they are no match for our ability to shift our attention. Even the most intense thoughts and feelings can fade and become irrelevant when we turn the spotlight off.

The key to maintaining new ways of thinking and new behaviors is to *remember* that we have the power to create our own experiences, despite what's happening in our day-to-day lives.

Creating a Climate for Change

Let's review the techniques that helped people successfully move through maintenance.

- *Commitment.* Once you've moved to the maintenance stage, you've controlled your environment, developed countering measures, and enlisted support. Dr. Prochaska and his colleagues say these successes can make you complacent without you even realizing it. Watch for warning signs. Beware of thoughts like "I'll skip my credit card payment this month" or "I will use my savings for this purchase, and put the money back later." It's the same as an alcoholic saying, "I'll have just one drink." It doesn't diminish your past successes, but it makes it awfully hard to get back on track.

- *Reward.* Giving yourself a treat or praise when you take that "road less traveled" will help build your self-esteem by reminding you of your accomplishments. Don't reward yourself, however, with things that will undermine your efforts. For example, don't save $100 and celebrate by going to Disneyland!

- *Helping relationships.* Stay connected with the people you've enlisted for support. Make sure they know you need their help when it comes to staying on course. You need them to confront you if you start reverting to old behavior, express overconfidence, expose yourself to tempting situations, or break any of the contracts you created during the previous stages of change.

- *Environment controls.* Keep avoiding the people, places, and things that could compromise your change efforts, especially in the early months of maintenance. This isn't about weakness. It's about having the strength to put yourself in the best possible environment for success. I'll share more tips on how to control your environment in just a moment.

- *Countering.* This can be very exciting! Make time for things and activities you've always wanted to do. Go to a yoga class once a week instead of going to the mall. Remember, Life Planning is about bringing your desires into your everyday life.

Pearls from Planners

"What you're essentially doing is developing muscles you didn't have before. For a time, you're going to have to do what does not come naturally. You're going to have to practice the nonhabitual. This involves things like saving money if you're a spender. Not 'overgiving' to your children, as so many of us tend to do. Lightening up, if you have a tendency to hoard money. You're going to have to do this with your thoughts as well as your actions. Stand back, and watch how these new thoughts and behaviors play out. It's extremely helpful to keep a journal. This lets you take time and check in with yourself—keep tabs on how it feels to build and flex those new muscles!"

Olivia Mellan, author, *Money Harmony: Resolving Money Conflicts in Your Life and Relationship* (New York: Walker and Company, 1994); psychotherapist; money coach; founder, Money Harmony.

Helping Yourself in Your Day-to-Day Life

We talked earlier about the challenges of *remembering* that you have the power to direct your attention to the beliefs and behaviors that will give you what you want—especially when you're caught up in the challenges of day-to-day life. Simple reminders can make all the difference.

These are some of tips Life Planners give their clients:

- *Keep your eye on the prize—stay connected to your goals.* Keep a picture of something that you're striving for in your wallet, where you'd normally keep your credit card. Maybe it's a picture of your dream house. Maybe it's a picture of your child who you want to send to college. This will make you pause and think before you make a purchase.

    Remember Dr. Prochaska's suggestion to keep a crisis card in your wallet or pocketbook with the following set of instructions:

    1. Review the problem.
    2. Substitute positive for negative thinking.
    3. Remember the benefits of change.
    4. Engage in rigorous distraction or exercise.
    5. Call your helper. Being a helper to someone with a similar problem is also helpful during the maintenance stage.

- *See relapses as learning experiences.* Falling off course is a great learning experience. You can learn where you are still vulnerable. Note the circumstance or event that triggered the relapse, and take note of what you were thinking before and during this little setback. Above all, don't let a relapse trigger a crisis of confidence or lower your self-esteem. Remind yourself of how far you've come, and give yourself a reward.

- *Get rid of clutter.* Life Planning is about getting rid of financial behaviors that don't help you achieve what matters most.
Planners say getting rid of things in your physical environment
that you don't need or that are no longer important goes a
long way in helping you do this in your financial life. Just as
we looked at your finances one at a time, go through each
room in your home. Take everything out of your drawers, clos-
ets, and cupboards, and put back only those things that you
use and need. If you're unsure, you probably don't need it.
This is also a great exercise to have your kids do once a month.
In addition, Planners say when you buy something new, make
sure you throw away the item it is replacing. Looking for more
ways to save money? Sell your things on eBay or have a tag sale.
Donating your things to charity is also a great way to stay connected with your true nature. It just feels good! So does the tax
deduction!
- *Keep some reminder of your goals in every room of your house.* This
can be pictures, lists, an image of a place you want to visit on
your screen saver, anything that reminds you of the things you
identified as your most important goals.
- *Keep track of your progress.* We often don't realize that we've successfully adjusted our behavior until we've made a new choice.
Take the time to notice, and congratulate yourself. As Paula
told you, your Bottom Line is a work in progress. You will
continue to make adjustments to your savings, investing, and
spending, as your financial circumstances change—you will
continue to move closer to your goals. Review and update your
Bottom Line at least every two weeks. This will also help you
reconnect to the goals and values that will guide you to your
dreams. Leave notes on your calendar, refrigerator, and so on,
to help you remember to do this. Also, use your helping relationships to help you maintain this new habit.
- *Helping others.* We've talked about the importance of philanthropy throughout this book. Volunteer and charity work not
only benefit others, but it also helps you keep your own life
in perspective. Remembering how lucky you are to have the
life that you've created is a great motivator when it comes to
maintaining it. In addition, see if there are people around
you trying to align their finances with their priorities. Helping
someone who can benefit from the things that you have gone

through not only feels good, but it also reminds you of your ability to change.

- *Get professional help.* All change comes from within. Therapists and counselors can, however, offer the guidance you need to keep marching forward on your journey. This is especially true when it comes to your finances. There are a lot of options out there when it comes to managing money. Professional help on some level is a necessity for most of us. We'll talk more about this shortly.

- *Self-checks.* We are bombarded by so many messages, scripts, and judgments from the outside world that it is no wonder that we rarely have time to hear and notice our own thoughts. As we've seen, however, those little "songs that play in our heads" guide much of our behavior. It is imperative to keep tabs on those tunes so that we can allow those that don't serve us to become distant melodies. Once a day, give yourself a "time-out," and check in on your thoughts. Review what you've been thinking about that day. Pay special attention to habitual thoughts. Stay connected to your goals, and identify financial behavior that may still be working against your priorities. See what comes up when you look at areas where you're still resisting change. You may need to go back to a previous change technique in order to move forward.

Body Reading

There is a growing science that works on the belief that there are specific areas of the body that react to different stresses and tension. Whether you fully accept it or not, it's interesting food for thought. Some people think it's an excellent way to keep tabs on what's going on in their thoughts and attitudes.

Pearls of Wisdom

"Emotion rises at the place where mind and body meet. It is the body's reaction to your mind or you might say a reflection of your mind in the body. For example, an attack thought, or a hostile thought, will create a build-up of energy in the body that we call anger. The body is

(Continued)

getting ready to fight. The thought that you are being threatened physically or psychologically causes the body to contract, and this is the physical side of what we call fear. Research has shown that strong emotions even cause changes in the biochemistry of the body. These biophysical changes represent the physical or material aspect of the emotion ... you will eventually experience them on a purely physical level, as a physical problem or symptom. ... If you really want to know your mind ... the body will always give you a truthful reflection."

Eckhart Tolle, *The Power of Now* (Vancouver, B.C.: Namaste Publishing, 1997).

Peter Smits is a Life Coach at the Good Life Spa in the Dutch West Indies, and an expert in body reading. He says that pain and tension in the following areas can be seen as warning signs that certain parts of your life need attention. See what you think!

- *Headaches.* Headaches mean that you are thinking, analyzing, and rationalizing too much. They can also mean that you need to become more focused. Your head literally hurts as it scrambles to make sense of too many scenarios. When you are too much in your head, you need to connect more with the physical body through exercise and activities.
- *Neck aches.* Pains in the neck have to do with communication. When you are experiencing these, you may notice that you're using a lot of statements of certainty in your language. Miscommunication comes from this inflexibility. You're holding onto old conditioned ways of communicating truths and beliefs. Stop speaking your own truths like they are a matter of public opinion. Stop being a pain in the neck to yourself and to others.
- *Shoulder pain.* The saying "The weight of the world is on my shoulders" is no exaggeration. People have known about body reading for a long time. Shoulder pains indicate that you are taking on too many burdens for yourself, and you're taking on the burdens of others or the world. Stop trying to control other people and situations. Free yourself. Conversely, shoulder pain can also come when you are avoiding responsibility. You will know the difference.

- *Spinal pain.* Bending over backwards, and turning and twisting yourself in too many directions, puts stress on your foundation—your spine. You will also experience spinal problems when you resist the natural twists and turns in life. This pain is warning us to stay more in the moment. Focus on what's *really happening* around you, not your *perceptions* of what you and other people should and shouldn't be doing. It is usually perceptions, not reality, that get us twisted.

- *Lower back pain.* You'll notice tension and pain in your lower back when you are racing into the future. Your body is your first line of protection. This area of your body is literally trying to hold you back. People also experience pain in this area when they are stuck and don't want to move forward at all. They are also going against the natural flow of life. Don't fight the forces of change. You're not strong enough. Good situations turn bad, and bad situations turn good. Don't resist them or fail to move with them.

- *Aches and pains in the upper legs.* The thighs tell us messages about our endurance. You may be losing strength and endurance to accomplish the things you want, or you may have strength and lack stamina and endurance. Deep breathing, exercise, and changes in diet and habits like smoking and drinking can help to build stamina and endurance.

- *Aches and pains in the knees.* Our knees are literally our shock absorbers. Pains in the knees mean that we are marching through life too stiffly, not bending to follow or absorbing the path that we are on. Don't forget your flexibility and your sense of humor.

- *Pain in the feet.* Pains in the feet have to do with security. We may be trying to find security where no security exists. We're trying to hold on to places, situations, and people where there is nothing. Spending time in nature and going for walks—activities connected with grounding—will help you regain your footing.

- *Chest pain.* You will experience chest pains when you are having trust issues. A trust has been betrayed, you're losing trust, losing heart, in others or yourself. There is some kind of emotional abrasion going on in your life. It is very important to slow down and take care of yourself when you have pain in this area. Always take care of your heart. Lots of deep breathing, quiet time, and rest. Also, make sure any betrayals of trust are not just your perceptions of a situation. Pain specifically in the breasts has to do with nurturing. Typically, we are not nurturing and nourishing ourselves, or we feel neglected. Breast pains also come when we are putting a lot of demands on ourselves to nourish and care for others.

- *Stomach pain.* You will notice pain and tightness in your stomach when you are having a hard time sorting things out—you are having difficulty in digesting and absorbing people, certain aspects of ourselves, and situations. Eat simple foods. Give the things in your life that have your stomach in knots, and yourself, rest, space, and time.

CHAPTER 21

Change Happens

After Sarah Roberts graduated college with a degree in political science, she did what her upper-middle-class family and society expected of her—she landed a good job as a consultant at an environmental consulting firm and set out to climb the corporate ladder.

A few years later, Sarah got married. She and her husband lived and worked in Washington, D.C., living what she calls "the typical D.C. lifestyle." She was working about 70 hours a week in her efforts to advance her career, and she spent a lot of her spare time thinking about work.

"We get so caught up in the work-and-spend cycle that we don't think about what really makes us happy. This job was bringing me a lot more stress than happiness," she told me.

The terrorist attacks on September 11, 2001, were one of several factors that made Sarah think that she should be spending more of her time doing the things that were really important to her. Spending a majority of her waking hours at a job she didn't really like so that she could pay for a lifestyle that wasn't helping her find a lot of happiness became a choice that was hard to live with.

"Some of the things I worried and cared about began to seem so unimportant. There are just more important things going on than working 70 hours a week. Even when I wasn't at work, I would spend a lot of time stressing about it. I didn't think I needed to be doing this anymore," she told me.

In addition, Sarah and her husband were looking at houses. Their search made them realize how much of a commitment they would have to make to their careers if they were to live in some of D.C.'s more affluent areas.

I'll get to how Sarah successfully changed her lifestyle in just a moment, but I think it's interesting to look at what was going on as she moved through this contemplation stage of change:

1. Her house hunt is a great example of consciousness raising, one of the techniques successful self-changers employ, which involves gathering information. She was able to see what living in certain neighborhoods would cost her in money and in time.
2. The events of September 11 generated the kind of emotional arousal that inspires change.
3. Her unhappiness at work, which was spilling over into other aspects of her life, made her think about how her life would be without that pressure. This is self-reevaluation.
4. In addition, her husband provided a helping relationship. She says he would really help her stay connected to her values and priorities, when she was thinking about the steps she could take to change her life. He also offered inspiration. Her husband worked at a company that allowed him to telecommute, meaning he could work from home, set his own schedule, and make time for things that he enjoyed doing.

These are the four techniques successful self-changers use to move out of contemplation. Sarah is a great example of a successful self-changer.

"I was able to deeply connect with the fact that more is not better. Once you're comfortable with who you are and what you want, you stop worrying about things like keeping up with your neighbors. That other stuff just falls away."

Sarah began looking for work that would let her live in sync with what was important to her. She wanted more time for herself, and she wanted to spend more time with her husband. Ironically, her search led her to a nonprofit organization that helps people bring their values into their spending and lifestyle. Not only did the work strike a special chord, but this company allowed her to work just four days a week. This resulted in a 53 percent drop in her income! Sarah was going to have to make some changes to her lifestyle.

For starters, she and her husband made the decision to buy a modest house, which they would take care of by themselves. They would no longer employ a housekeeper. They also cut their expenses by getting rid of a car, using public transportation, and cutting back on some of their social outings.

"It wasn't hard. You have limitations and you live within those boundaries. We were so much happier that those things became easy."

"The key is figuring out what you really want, so that you can be happy with your decisions. They have to be right for you. You can't just stop once you've set these changes in motion. If you make the right choices, your new lifestyle won't be hard to maintain. You'll be happy, so you won't second-guess yourself."

I recently caught up with Sarah, as she and her husband were in the process of moving to New Jersey. He got a promotion. The timing was good. They recently had a child, and Sarah had stopped working altogether. It was easy for her to pick up and move.

"Once you make the decision to let your values guide your choices, things fall into place," she told me.

An Extra Set of Eyes

Many of us need help remembering the goals and values that should be driving our decisions. Our scripts, experiences, and lifestyles can make us lose sight of who we really are.

Life Planners have shown how the right professional help can be just the reminder we need.

Rick and Linda Long had many scripts that didn't allow them to see the choices they needed to make to bring them the life they really wanted.

Rick's father and grandfather were gambling addicts. His parents divorced when he was very young, and his mother remarried into a middle-class family Rick calls "scarcity conscious."

Linda's father was a banker. There was a lot of accountability required when it came to her financial choices. In addition, her mother made all of the decisions about the family finances. Linda rebelled by doing a lot of "get back at you" spending.

These lessons had a big impact on Rick and Linda's financial behavior. Both of them had first marriages that ended in divorce, due in part to the stresses that came with heavy levels of debt.

When Rick and Linda got married in 1986, these patterns were still there. They filed for bankruptcy within the first 18 months of their marriage.

Rick made a nice salary as a therapist. Since he was paid by the hour, he would often try and predict his income. He said he'd write checks on the expectation that the business would come.

This resulted in payments of between $400 and $500 a month in fees to his bank for bouncing checks. Rick says his betting on future income was a form of gambling—he was doing the same thing his father and grandfather did.

In addition, he was doing the same thing as his father when it came to controlling the family finances. He would spend money without consulting Linda, feeling like he deserved it. He made the most money. She was a counselor at an elementary school.

Linda did what she knew. She stayed away from the financial decisions, but would spend to get back at Rick for controlling her money and making her account for how she used it.

A few years ago, Rick was lucky enough to meet psychologist Ted Klonz through a mutual friend. (Ted shared his personal story with you in Chapter 6.) Rick told Ted his financial issues, and Ted directed him to his partner, financial planner Rick Kahler. They've combined their skills to create one of the most successful Life Planning practices in the country.

Rick told me that when he met Mr. Kahler, he said one word that changed his life. He told the couple they needed to restore *integrity* to their financial behavior.

"It was like a light was turned on. It had never occurred to me to look at integrity in our finances," Rick told me.

"Linda and I made vows to respect each other and act with integrity when it comes to elements of our marriage like fidelity. Finances are simply another aspect of the total relationship. When you vow to treat someone with respect, it's across the board. When Rick Kahler helped me see this, it really changed my life," he added.

Kahler helped Linda discover how much she resented always having to ask for what she needed and having someone else control her money. This awareness allowed her to bring a new level of maturity to her financial decisions.

Through self-reevaluation and Rick Kahler's helping relationship and expertise in preparing them for the changes they wanted to make, this couple was able to move to the action stage of change. They radically transformed their financial behavior in a way that reflects who they really are—two people with a great deal of integrity and a tremendous amount of love and respect for one another.

"We haven't bounced a check in a year and a half. We have a budget and disclose what we are spending, and we helped Linda with her control issues by giving her control of the family finances. It was a big move, but it's given her a sense of confidence that she never had before."

"Changing your financial behavior is not an easy thing. Based on our experience, we would tell couples they have to get honest, and look at the idea that money is a real part of their relationship. People must realize that money is the aspect of a relationship where power struggles and unfinished business play out. It must be looked at if you are going to have trust and intimacy in the other areas."

Rick and Linda were lucky to find the type of help they needed to change their financial behavior. In the next chapter we'll discuss the best places for you to go for professional help as you move through the change process.

CHAPTER 22

Getting the Help You Need

Throughout this book we've talked about professional help as being part of the change process, and not the catalyst for change itself. Even if you spend as much as two hours a week with a counselor or therapist, you're still on your own for the remaining 166 hours!

People tend to spend even less time with financial planners—maybe just a few hours a year. That's why it's so important to empower yourself with knowledge about your finances. It's up to you to execute the financial plan—you will be responsible for your actions.

The good news is that it has never been easier to get financial information. There are 24-hour news channels devoted to business and money. Business and personal finance reports have taken on a bigger role in local and national news—particularly since the stock market boom dominated the headlines in the late 1990s. Web sites like SmartMoney.com, MarketWatch.com, and Kiplinger.com keep you updated on the latest financial news, allow you to track your investments, and offer extensive personal financial advice for free.

Still, managing money has become a complicated business. I urge you to get professional financial checkups at least once a year, to help you keep your plan on track. As we've seen, however, there are a lot of forces at work when it comes to your financial behavior. That means you now have to consider the following two factors in your search for professional help with your finances:

1. The professional's financial background.
2. Whether this person can help you with the nonfinancial side of your financial behavior.

Mindful Money Management Is Catching On

The personal finance industry is acknowledging the fact that planners must consider their clients' goals and priorities if they are going to successfully help them make the best financial choices—the kinds of choices that will keep them coming back for more guidance.

Being a financial reporter has allowed me to see this shift in the industry's focus firsthand. Personal finance experts are putting more and more emphasis on helping people to identify their life aspirations. Take a look at some of the latest ads from the big financial firms. Planners are at their clients' weddings, dinner tables, even sitting with them at intimate locations, like beaches, while they reflect on the things that will make them truly happy.

At the Financial Planning Association's annual meeting—the biggest annual event for the industry, where standards and guidelines are determined—Life Planning, or mindful money management, as some professionals prefer to call it, is becoming a regular part of key discussions and training.

As is the case with most industries, the product is being driven by public demand.

There has been a shift in the public's attitudes about money in the post-9/11 world. Quality of life has become more important than ever.

It's up to planners to incorporate this new reality into their practices. Still, as Marty Carter, a licensed family counselor who specializes in financial behavior, once told me, "We should not be opening wounds that we are not trained to help people heal."

Emotional and psychological issues will come up when you set out to align your finances with your values. Let's make sure that you hire someone who can help you with the total picture.

Finding the Right Help

You are going to be one well-informed client! You've learned enough about the complex aspects of financial management to walk into a financial planner's office and not only tell them the goals you want your finances to support, but you can also tell them about the habits and tendencies that may be standing in your way. You may decide that you only need help with the financial side of the equation, or you may want someone whose trained to take your financial personality into account.

The following guidelines will help you find the right person:

- *Check their qualifications.* Anyone can call himself a financial planner. You want to make sure the person you hire has earned credentials as a CFP (certified financial planner)—they must have a bachelor's degree (starting in 2007), have five years of experience, and they must have passed an exam. There is also a PFS (personal financial specialist) credential. These are given to certified public accountants (CPAs) with a certain degree of financial knowledge. They tend to emphasize taxes and accounting.
- *Find out the types of services they provide.* Not all planners offer comprehensive services or a wide range of products. Some focus on specific areas of finance, like investing or estate planning. Be sure that you're clear on the type of advice you will be receiving and the financial vehicles at your disposal. Some planners will only offer advice. It's up to you to execute the plan. Also, find out how many different people you'll be working with and what they each bring to the process. You also want the planner to provide a detailed breakdown of all of the costs you'll incur. (We'll talk more about what you can expect to pay in just a moment.) In addition, find out if the planner is willing to give you a written agreement. You really want to think about your needs and make sure you align yourself with someone who can meet them.
- *Find out how they get paid for the services they provide.* There are generally three compensation models:
  1. **Fee-only planners.** They don't get a commission for the products they sell. Still, ask them if they have any relationship with or are compensated in any way by the companies whose products they offer. These planners generally get their compensation for the advice they give, but they may receive outside monies. Ask. Many of the planners I've met who practice Life Planning and mindful money management fall into this category.
  2. **Fee-based planners.** They may receive a commission on some products in addition to the money they receive for the advice they give. You should find out what these planners get paid from these outside firms and what they get from their employer. (They may be self-employed.) Also ask if

they are compensated for getting you to use a particular financial product from the financial service firms they use—do they get an extra perk each time they sell stock X or mutual fund Y? You're trying to get an idea of where their financial motivation is coming from, so that you can asses if it's working in your best interests.

3. **Commission-based planners.** They are compensated by the companies whose products they sell. They don't get paid for their time or advice. They will not make a dime unless they sell a certain company's product. Use your instincts when it comes to evaluating these planners.

- *Ask about the things they consider when they help clients make financial choices.* See if their recommendations are based on the client's personal goals, or if they just look at their financial needs. See if they bring up the fact that financial choices are rooted in more complex issues. If they don't, ask them what they think of these theories. A growing number of planners are actually getting training in helping their clients identify their goals, and working with the factors that drive their behavior. Ask if they've had any such training, or if they have ever referred clients to people who can help them with these issues—more and more planners are employing professionals on their staffs with training in psychology and psychotherapy. Again, you may feel confident in your own abilities to help a planner see your goals and nonfinancial needs. See if they have a willingness to go down this road and if what they're saying makes you comfortable.

- *Tell them about your goals, and ask them the financial strategies they would use to help you achieve them.* You not only want to hear them describe a diversified portfolio that takes your age and time horizon for achieving your goals into consideration, but you also want them to consider your financial behavior patterns. For example, it would be helpful to have a planner put a chunk of your savings into a certificate of deposit (CD) or other short-term investment, where you can't easily get your hands on it, if you have a tendency to overspend.

- *Get references.* Ask the planner to give you the names of three clients. (Keep in mind that they will likely have a good personal relationship with these people.) Ask the clients specific questions about the financial results this planner has brought them when it comes to achieving their goals. Ask about the factors they allowed to drive the financial decisions. Did their goals and values come into play? Friends and family are a great resource for references. Just understand that you may have different needs and different expectations for your planner. The Certified Financial Planning Board of Standards (www.cfp.net) and the Financial Planning Association (www.fpanet.org) can provide references and referrals. You can also find out if a planner has ever been charged with disciplinary action at the Financial Planning Association site.

- *Compare your options.* Talk to at least three planners. See if they meet your needs and if you're comfortable with their personal style.
- *Trust your judgment.* Make sure that you and this person have compatible communication styles. Is he comfortable when you ask the "tough questions"? Is this someone who you would be comfortable opening up to about some of the factors that are behind your financial choices? He is the professional. It's up to him to give you a high level of comfort in his financial and communication skills.

Where to Find a Planner

If you decide you just need help on the financial side, The Certified Financial Planning Board of Standards (www.cfp.net) and the Financial Planning Association (www.fpanet.org) can help you locate planners in your area.

The Yellow Pages and a search on the Internet can also help you locate the right person.

For a fee, a Web site called MyFinancialAdvice.com, will help you find a planner in your area and interview him or her live, via Internet chat, or phone. This is a great service, but you may still want the benefits of a face-to-face encounter.

There are also a growing number of therapists and psychologists who focus on financial issues. Finding one will require some research. Use the same criteria we discussed for picking a financial planner. Many of these professionals, however, do not get involved in the financial planning process at all—it's not their specialty. Make sure that you are clear on whether they can direct you to the financial expertise you need—many work with financial advisers.

Costs

George Kinder, who is considered by many to be one of the founders of the Life Planning movement (we used his exercise in Chapter 3 to help you identify your goals), has put together a national database of planners who practice Life Planning on his Web site at www.kinder-institute.com. You can see if there are any in your area.

You can typically expect to pay anywhere between $120 and $350 an hour. Many charge a percentage of your total net worth—typically 1 to 2.5 percent.

The College for Financial Planner got the following results when they surveyed CFPs about their costs:

- Five percent charge less than $100 an hour.
- Fifty-one percent charge between $100 and $199 an hour.
- Thirty-seven percent charge between $200 and $299 an hour.
- Four percent charge between $300 and $399 an hour.
- One percent charge between $400 and $499 an hour.
- Two percent charge $500 an hour.

Fees may be higher for planners who've been in the field longer, or for planners with specialties like high-net-worth estate planning.

A Helping Relationship

You may decide that you need help with the change process itself. You may need assistance getting to that the point where you can make the adjustments to your behavior that will make your goals a reality.

Spiritual advisers, counselors, psychotherapists, psychiatrists, and psychologists, particularly those who focus on the financial field, can offer the helping relationship you need. Again, finding these people will take some research on your part.

Anyone can call himself a counselor or a therapist. Be very clear on what the individual brings to the table before you employ someone without a professional degree—you should know a great deal about the person you are dealing with. Psychologists usually have doctoral degrees and have done internships. Psychiatrists are physicians who've done residencies in psychiatry. They are the only mental health professionals who can prescribe medication. You may have insurance that covers all or part of these costs.

The following guidelines can help you determine if you want to consider this type of support:

- Your relapses are becoming more frequent instead of lessening.
- Long-term patterns won't budge despite awareness of the problem and persistent efforts to change them.
- You have a tendency to replace destructive behavior patterns with destructive behavior patterns.
- You have a hard time understanding where you are in the change process.
- You know where you are and what techniques to apply, but you just can't bring yourself to do it.
- You don't have many helping relationships in your life.

A Final Thought

The idea for this book came out of a sense of journalistic responsibility and Paula's desire to give people the financial tools they need to live out their dreams. As I reflect on my own life, journalism—getting people information that will help them live better lives—is one of my greatest passions. When I came across Life Planning, I knew that this was one of the most important things that I could ever share. That led me on a long journey that has greatly enhanced my own life. I hope with all of my heart that the information that Paula and I put together in this book does the same for you. I hope it helps you find *true happiness.* Thank you for being my inspiration for this story.

Index